Quintessential Redneck

Wesley Whisenhunt

WestBow
PRESS®
A DIVISION OF THOMAS NELSON
& ZONDERVAN

WestBow Press books may be ordered through booksellers or by contacting:

WestBow Press
A Division of Thomas Nelson & Zondervan
1663 Liberty Drive
Bloomington, IN 47403
www.westbowpress.com
1 (866) 928-1240

ISBN: 978-1-9736-0807-3 (sc)
ISBN: 978-1-9736-0808-0 (e)

Print information available on the last page.

WestBow Press rev. date: 12/7/2017

To Amanda, Denver and Casey
"More than a whole herd of dead buffalo"
I love you for as long as grass grows and wind blows.
And even longer if that is possible …

———————— • ————————

To my guardian angel.
Thanks for working overtime.

PROLOGUE

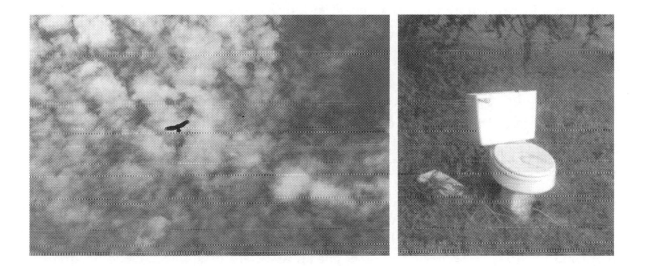

No doubt about it: the day I pitched my commode off my front porch was a watershed event in my life. I guess the first part of the epiphany was how calm and satisfied I felt while tossing a cracked toilet bowl out in my front yard. The second part was that in doing that act, I proved I was a quintessential redneck.

And as I did the act the thought hit me: how could I possibly be a redneck if I knew the word quintessential … or epiphany?

I was a forty-something-year-old, and still considered myself a late twenty-something-year-old, and a work in progress. My wife and I were living on an eighteen-acre place about six miles east of Holland, Texas. I believe it was a warm spring day, but don't hold me to that. I almost had to laugh at my deed. Doing what I'd just done was a brand-new low—or better put, a brand-new realization on a different level—of who I was now, the *quintessential-ness* of it, so to speak (if that's a word). Most people would have hired a plumber to fix the thing, or had a garage to put it in, but I had neither.

But it didn't matter. I was a Texan, born and bred, and I was free.

After all, really, what was there to be ashamed of? My mobile home was aging but well-constructed, and anchored better than some site-built homes. The red neck I sport to this day (and there really is such a thing, occurring when a person literally spends years outside) was a result of hard honest work and other activities outdoors in the wide-open spaces. To my thinking, country life was much more wholesome than city dwelling. And so, what I'd tossed a toilet off my porch? It wasn't like there were any neighbors close by who could see it, now forlornly sitting there at an angle in the front yard. Plus, I fully intended to throw it away at a more convenient time. So, truth be told, it was no skin off anybody's nose but mine.

But that begs the question: how did I get here, to this point? Hopefully this book will explore the origin of the answer to that question. More, it will explore how we all—every man-jack and woman-jill of us who experienced that weird decade called the 1960s—came to various strange junctures in our lives. It may also be a description of that inner child in me that just happened to form in the 1960s.

But first, to understand how a reasonably normal man ended up throwing a large piece of ceramic plumbing into his yard, maybe I should tell you a little bit about who Wes Whisenhunt is … and as the cowboy Curley said in the musical *Oklahoma*, "How did I get to be the way I ere?"

Growing up I didn't know how poor we were. My mom says that when they got married in 1955 they only had fifty dollars total; in other words, she had fifty and Daddy had zero. Daddy farmed and went to G.I. school at night.

I worked very many years in the electronics manufacturing industry. I graduated from high school in 1976, and in 1978 got an associate of applied science degree in electronics. Three years later, in 1981, I bought some land, but I was really unsure if I knew enough to live in the country, although that was what I wanted to do, more than anything. I suppose I come by that outlook honestly. In my late twenties, I'd come across an accountant who was the biggest nerd you ever met, but he lived in the country and ran livestock.

And that chewed at me. Day and night.

Right there and right then I decided that if Abe the numbers geek could do the country thing, I could too. But I didn't get the chance. Due to work slowdown, I transferred to Austin. There I found myself doing the bachelor scene—which wasn't as wild and partying and carefree as you might think—and working swing shift at an electronics company. But all in all, things were manageable. I'd rented a nice one-bedroom apartment, had fairly sturdy furniture, and owned two good cars. One was a Ford Escort, the other a Ford pickup (I guess it's true: you can take the boy outta the country, but you can't take the country outta the boy).

But then work slowed down again, and things got tight. Eventually I was forced to move to a ten by twelve portable building on the eighteen acres of land I'd bought years before, in 1981. I continued to work in electronics, but prepared for a lay-off that never came. One good thing though, I met my wife Patricia in Austin, and after our marriage in 1989, we moved to a neighbor's mobile home next to a barn.

As I said, I continued to work at my electronics job, at the same time toiling on a neighbor's ranch for the mobile home rent. Still, hard as I hammered at it, I couldn't get away from … me. Even with all that daily backbreaking, blister-raising effort I still viewed myself as a bumbling nerd trying to be a cowboy. Eighteen months after that Tricia and I bought a double-wide, and moved to our eighteen acres.

All the while I toiled away at my electronics job, hoping for a balance between town and country life. But the taste I'd gotten of living that country life always made me want more of it. Once again work slowed down, and this time we left Texas and moved to Oregon. It was a have-to thing, but looking back, the necessity of that move didn't make it any easier. The people up there were nice enough people, but I really enjoyed jerking their chain.

Don't ask me why, but it seemed everyone in Oregon saw me as some kind a cross between Hank Hill and the Unabomber. I guess that's because I used to tell them nothing was wrong with their state that couldn't be fixed with a chain saw and dynamite. How to win friends and influence people, right? There was just no helping it: I didn't fit in, and I really missed the flat land I grew up in.

Oregon made me feel claustrophobic. The mountains and trees, while magnificent, caused me to feel uncomfortable, and birthed in me a longing for the wide-open Texas skies I'd known and loved as a boy. As a kid, I used to lie on the ground and look at the clouds. Sometimes when there were no clouds you could get the sensation you were falling up because there was no point of reference (and perhaps due to an over-active imagination). All that big sky made me feel closer to God. I got a sense of how small I was, and how big He was.

To my thinking, if Oregon were flatter, it would be a better place.

And then in 1998, our chance came. A job opened up, and we moved back to Texas. Yee-ha and praise the Lord. We felt the chains slipping away, like the children of Israel coming into the Promised Land. Thankfully I'd kept the eighteen acres and the double wide. Before leaving I'd converted it to rental property, and now after moving back, I changed it back to our place of abode.

And I needed that sense of belonging now that once again I was working with much-younger-than-me computer geeks. While they would spend their precious weekends constructing home theater systems for their houses or rebuilding their computers, I was putting up steel goat fences, hauling hay, and shredding pastures. Worlds apart, I know, but that's simply how things were. And now that my mobile home was getting long in the tooth, having endured another family, the bathrooms were in dire need of some upgrades. That job fell to me.

That afternoon as I tossed the toilet in the front yard, to be hauled off later, I guess it hit me. At long last I finally realized that I truly wasn't like my co-workers in the electronics industry, and never would be. Years ago, something had bit me hard while I was living on the plains of Arnett, Texas, and there was no cure.

What does all this have to do with throwing my commode off the front porch? Well, most people live in the city and are worried what the neighbors would think, or worried about a city ordinance or something when removing a porcelain throne whose replacement time had come. Since I do not have any neighbors that can see my house or not enough resources to hire a plumber or a garage to place the toilet in to hide from sight until someone can come and haul it away, I fall into that category known as redneck, a word that has evolved in meaning, and ever-changing definition based on the individual's past history and environment.

It once was a word that many men wore with pride. I know I did growing up, although most simply called it a farmer's tan. A redneck was one that spent a lot of time outdoors with their clothes on, working hard and receiving permanent skin damage on those parts of the body that failed to receive protection. It was not fully understood as skin damage, sometimes not understood at all.

I once thought that if you conditioned your body, you could get to the point where you no longer got burned. The neck was that part of the body that reached that pinnacle of success, not by choice, but by the sheer fact that no article of clothing truly protected it while one was outside earning an honest day's wages for an honest day's work.

A red neck was a badge of honor. It meant you weren't afraid of hard work and had the mark to prove it. You weren't soft; you'd stood up to the test and had been kissed by the sun. Contrariwise, the rest of you was white as alabaster and indicated that you had not spent a great deal of time with little clothing on swimming or sun bathing, both recreational activities that could only be done if you were idle.

Somewhere along the way the term became a derogatory word for stupidity and ignorance. It became a word one redneck could say to another without offense, but was reason for a fight if called that by one that didn't have a red neck (I guess it's not unlike blacks calling each other "nigga", but getting offended if called such by a Caucasian).

Nonetheless, I'm a redneck, and that's all there is to it. I have the permanently damaged skin to prove my label, skin that only changes in shade, and almost never burns. I have little money, and I'm surely considered stupid by most for living in a mobile home for over a decade, a man capable of tossing his toilet out in the front yard.

But it doesn't matter. My neck is red and my Texan blood, if spilt on the ground, would cry to the heavens "Don't fence me in." That day as I tossed that toilet out onto the lawn, right there in front of God and myself there was a release, a freeing. With that act of rebellion came the knowledge that, as Popeye put it, "I yam what I yam."

And the rebel in me lives on. At the time I started this writing, I still worked with a vast number of people who were not native Texans. Or if they *were* natives, they grew up in towns or cities, and not out in the wide-open spaces like me. Almost none of them are old enough to remember outdoor toilets, drive-in movies, or *Have Gun Will Travel* (with that deadly gun-for-hire, Paladin) on the TV. Very few of them lived in such sparse populations where they could even think outside the box. And that's a shame.

Today people are guided by homeowners' associations and city ordinances and endless restrictions that restrict and impede their every movement. They're mind-numbed automatons, so locked into their rules and regulations they could never, not in their wildest dreams, ever conceive of tossing a commode off the front porch.

And that's too bad for them. For me, it was a liberating experience. Because I know who I am now. For good or for bad, I'm me. And I'm okay.

I'm also not going to talk a lot about my wife and kids; they aren't germane to the purpose of this book, but I'll say this. One of my favorite movie lines comes from *Little Big Man*, with Dustin Hoffman. I can't recall the exact context, but the line is, "as long as the wind blows and the grass grows." I interpret this to mean, "as long as the earth exists." One of my most endearing words to another is, "I'll love you as long as the wind blows and the grass grows."

Before I forget, I'd like to mention the odd phrase within the dedication placed at the beginning of this memoir (I know some of you are scratching your head over it; I would). Years ago, a movie came out called *The Life and Times of Evil Roy Slade*, starring John Astin. The premise was a hoot. As I remember it, Evil Roy had been abandoned as a child, and then raised by a flock of buzzards (work with me here; this is good).

Later in life Roy became an outlaw, and then after he was apprehended, he became a shoe salesman. It was then he fell in love with a beautiful girl. While trying to explain his emotions to the buzzards that'd raised him (I told you to work with me here), he used a term he knew they'd understand. He says, "When I'm with her I feel like I'm in heaven. But since you don't know what heaven is like, I'll describe it. It's like a whole herd of dead buffalo."

Since family should make me feel like I'm in heaven, and since I'm really nothing more than a cranky old buzzard anyway, I often tell many of them I love them "more than a whole herd of dead buffalo." Oddly enough, they've never really found any satisfaction in this phrase of my undying affection. Go figure.

Being a child of the prairie, in my mind there's a connection to "grass growing and wind blowing" and buffalo and buzzards. I don't know, maybe that's a bit of a stretch for most people to get. But to me it makes sense, and is funny in my mind.

But as to this book, let's begin.

Onward to the Sixties.

CHAPTER ONE

◆

1960

The 1960s decade refers to the years from the beginning of 1960 to the end of 1969, and that's pretty much what this book will cover. The term also refers to an era more often called "the Sixties". It was a time of complex inter-related cultural and political trends which occurred roughly during the years 1963-1973 in the west, particularly Britain, France, Canada, Australia, Italy and West Germany ... and of course the good old USA.

If you lived through the 60s, you already know what a wild time it was; my relating the events of those years won't make them more real. But if you didn't, I'm going to tell you. And it may well-nigh sound unbelievable. So strap down and hang on. Because make no mistake: the Sixties were one mean ride.

Although the calendar says the decade started in 1960, in the United States the Sixties really lasted from about 1963 to 1973; to a lot of folks the first three years were just a holdover from the Fifties, and were the preliminary bout for the main event. In 1960 the population was 177,830,000, and of these an estimated 850,000 "war baby" freshmen entered college that year. In fact there were so many of them doing so that emergency living quarters had to be set up in dorm lounges, hotels and trailer camps.

Some facts about the Sixties: the average salary was $4,473, while teachers on the average made a bit more than that, coming in right at $5,174 … which wasn't too bad, considering the minimum wage was a measly buck an hour! The national debt was only $286 billion, and I say "only" because we recently spent over twice that *in one day* to bail out our banking system. Life expectancy then for males was 66.6 years; for females it was a shade longer, 73.1 years.

Some pundits also label the time the "Swinging Sixties", because of the do-whatever-you-like attitudes that seemed to emerge like locusts from cocoons during this decade. The phrase "do your own thing" was birthed then, and pretty much sums up the thinking of many during that time. Rampant drug use has become inextricably associated with the counter-culture of the era, and in many people's minds the 1960s have become synonymous with all the new, exciting, radical, and subversive events and trends of the period, trends which continued to develop in the 70s, 80s, 90s and beyond … even in Texas. American automobile manufacturers evolved the streamlined, jet-inspired design for sports cars, coming up with sleek classics such as the Pontiac GTO, the Plymouth Barracuda, the Ford Mustang, and the Chevrolet Corvette.

Younger generations soon began to rebel against the conservative norms of the time, as well as disassociate themselves from mainstream liberalism. In particular they turned away from the high levels of materialism which was so common during the era. This created a counter-culture that eventually turned into a social revolution throughout much of the western world. This movement was marked by wide-spread drug use (including LSD, peyote, and marijuana) and psychedelic music.

In the United States, it began as a reaction against the conservative social norms and stasis of the 1950s, the perceived political conservatism (and social repression) of the Cold War period, and the US government's extensive military intervention in Vietnam. The more socially-aware, culturally "with-it" youth from the movement were called hippies. We saw these strange people on news reports on the TV, but they had very little impact on our small Texas worldviews … at first anyway. Together the hippies created a new, liberated (to their minds) stance for society, a wide-openness that included the sexual revolution, questioning authority and government, and demanding more freedoms and rights for women, homosexuals, and minorities.

The 1960s didn't start out with colorful clothes. The duds were dully designed, and truthfully looked better on older people … which it seemed to me we had a lot of in our town. And lots of times you'd find those old folks in stores. I remember Gatesville having stores, but malls had yet to catch on, at least where we lived.

Until 1962 or thereabouts there was a carry over from the 50s, including the "bouffant" look, consisting of a dress where the top part is tight and the skirt of the dress puffs out. The popular hairstyle was a beehive, where they teased their hair and piled it high on their head. The 1960s began with crew cuts on men, but that didn't last. Men's casual shirts were often plaid and buttoned down the front, while knee-length dresses were required wear for women in most public places.

Another look during this time was the beatnik. The beat look included black berets, black slacks (tight for women) and dark glasses. Women wore float shoes and dark eye makeup while men wore sandals. Then little shops called boutiques opened selling cheap and colorful clothing for younger people. About this time space-age clothing started to become popular. Different materials were used, such as leather, discs of metal or plastic linked together with wire. Metallic or neon colors were involved. I guess "space-age" *is* the correct term, because when we saw these critters on the news, we all thought they looked like they were birthed on another planet.

By the following year, 1963, French designer Pierre Cardin had come up with the famous Beatles suits, which became popular for men. The suit had a single breasted collarless jacket and slim pants. Fashion guru Mary Quant started her own label, and was responsible for designing miniskirts, colored tights, and wet look vinyl fashions. By mid-decade, miniskirts or hot pants—often worn with go-go boots—were revealing legs, body wear was revealing curves, and women's hair was either very short or long and lanky.

Men's hair became longer and wider, along with beards and moustaches becoming popular. Menswear also had a renaissance of sorts. Bright colors, double-breasted sports jackets, tie-dyed tee shirts, polyester pants suits with Nehru jackets, and turtlenecks started to be in vogue. By the end of the decade men's ties, when worn, were up to three or four inches wide, and patterned, even when worn with stripes. Blacks of both genders began fixing their hair in an afro.

Women wore peasant skirts or granny dresses and chunky shoes. Unisex dressing was popular, featuring bell-bottomed jeans, love beads, and embellished t-shirts. Clothing was as likely to be purchased at surplus stores as boutiques. Bold, solid color contrasts came from the Op Art and Pop Art movements, commonly called Mod fashions.

During the decade, along with their miniskirts women started wearing leather boots and fake eyelashes. Men began sporting paisley shirts, velvet trousers and high collared "Regency" jackets; they also started wearing their hair longer. Miniskirts became much shorter, and Op Art clothing (an optic trick using contrasting colors with black and white to make a sort of optical illusion) became more popular.

By 1966 psychedelic clothing was now a hit. This was clothing with acid-like colors to make them brighter and bolder. Men begin to dress "fancy". Ethnic fashions began to spread, with the look coming from clothing picked up from other cultures. The Oriental look and the African/Middle Eastern looks were both part of the ethnic fashion.

By the end of the 60s skirts began to lengthen out, along with hair. The "hippie look" was now popular. The women wore long floor length dresses and skirts called maxies. Men continued to grow their hair longer as hippies decorated everything, including painting their bodies.

I can't tell you how little we Texans thought of this nuttiness. It was if the clothing and hair fashions were signaling a sea-change in the whole culture, a change we were ill-equipped to handle.

As the decade ground on even weirder stuff started showing up in the big cities; we held an equally dim view of this as well. The "underground press", a wide-spread, eclectic collection of small student newspapers usually printed off in small batches in garages or basements also started in the 60s, and served as a unifying factor for the counterculture.

Movies didn't escape the decade unscathed either. The Counterculture Revolution had a big effect on cinema. Movies began to break social taboos such as sex and violence, causing both controversy and fascination. They turned increasingly dramatic, unbalanced, and hectic as the cultural revolution was starting. This was the beginning of the New Hollywood era that dominated the next decade in theatres and revolutionized the movie industry. In Gatesville, Texas, we didn't know what to make of it all.

Films such as Arthur Penn's *Bonnie and Clyde* (1967), Stanley Kubrick's *2001: A Space Odyssey* (1968), and Roman Polanski's *Rosemary's Baby* (1968) are examples of this new, edgy direction. Films of this time also focused on the changes happening in the world. Dennis Hopper's *Easy Rider* (1969) focused on the drug culture of the time. Movies also became more sexually explicit, such as Roger Vadim's *Barbarella* (1968), as the counterculture progressed. I can tell you for sure the citizens of our town didn't hold with such stuff. But the times were changing, and unwillingly we were swept along.

In Europe, Art Cinema gained wider distribution and saw movements like la Nouvelle Vague (The French New Wave), the Cinéma Vérité documentary movement in Canada, France and the United States, and the high-point of Italian filmmaking with such artisans as Michelangelo Antonioni, Federico Fellini and Pier Paulo Pasolini making some of their most known films during this period (not that I saw any ... or wanted to).

Likewise, sports records fell in the Sixties. I know that sounds self-evident, as sports records are always falling, but the decade saw some new stuff. For instance, in 1962 Jackie Robinson, the first black American to have played in major league baseball, was placed in the Baseball Hall of Fame for his talent. Roger Maris hit homer number 61, setting a record that wasn't broken until the September of 1998 by Mark McGwire. Also the first Super Bowl was played in 1967, with the Green Bay Packers and the Kansas City Chiefs; the Packers won. And in 1965 the world's first roofed stadium was built, the Houston Astrodome (and what *was* this new "Astroturf" stuff anyway?).

Looking back on 1960, the world was poor. I don't mean monetarily, although I know many countries were, and still are, so bereft of folding cash they "don't have a pot to use for a toilet" (as we say in Texas, when we are avoiding profane language but trying to describe really poor). No, I mean the world was poor in things we take for granted today. Things like cell phones, computers, the Internet, X-box game players, microwave ovens, central heat, central air conditioning, cable TV, permanent press clothes …

Of course, they didn't know they were lacking in those items (not having been invented yet). If you would have asked the typical sun-baked resident of 1960 Gatesville, Texas if they missed not being able to watch Jay Leno on the cable, you most likely would have gotten a puzzled earthy comment, a gimlet eye, and a brown stream of Red Man tobacco juice directed toward your left boot (you *were* wearing boots, weren't you? As Merle Haggard said in *Okie from Muskogee*, they're the manly thing in footwear).

Truthfully, most men smoked and some old women dipped snuff, so with boots you might have been safe, but rest assured people would not have recognized Jay Leno as even being a name of a person. If they had, they'd still be puzzled as to what kind of cable he was using, or why he was using it; most people used heavy chains to pull cars or tractors out of mud holes instead of cables.

And as the Year of Our Lord 1960 dawned, I personally couldn't have cared less about those things either. At two and a half years old, my world consisted of my dad Charles, my mom Jo Dean, our red hound dog Skippy, and enough Cheerios and milk to keep the wheels lubed (my dad used to call me the Cheerio Kid as we play-wrestled on the floor). The Sixties were a wrestling match as well, not only for me but for the nation.

Everyone struggled with who they were and who they wanted to be; perhaps this is true in every decade.

I told you before what we didn't have, living on farm seven miles west of town. But what we had was better. Things city folks call silly, and corny, and not worthy of comment. Items like family picnics, pick-up baseball games (I was, a big baseball fan), long, lazy summer evenings sipping tall cool glasses of lemonade while sitting on the porch listening to crickets and Gulf coast toads, dinner on the grounds after church on Sunday, love of community, and love of God. The workaday events that seem so painfully quaint today were our life's blood then.

What I'm going to do in this book is relate some of those happenings. I hope to try to evoke a time that's passed, but whose effects linger on.

Here's the thing: I once wrote a poem which contained the line, "I'm not a prophet, a priest, or a sage; I'm just a man who bleeds on a page." My bloodletting is somewhat therapeutic for me, and hopefully beneficial to those who read these words. So that's what I'm going to do here.

As we go, I'll speak of world events both large and small, and how they affected a small boy and his family growing up outside a small Texas town in the 1960s. I'm going to address head-on the issues that tore this country apart. Things like racism, politics, the Vietnam War, sex, drugs, rock and roll, the whole enchilada. And maybe, just maybe, my telling of these things will give somebody somewhere some workable ideas on where we're going now.

Social and political upheaval was everywhere, not just here in the good old USA (in the United States, if you want to be culturally technical), but the entire world. As I said the Sixties really lasted from about 1963 to 1973; things didn't really get strange until after President Kennedy got shot.

After that, it was the decade that didn't know when to quit.

The term is three-fold. It's used descriptively by the media and history types; with fond nostalgia by those "long-haired hippies" birthed then (those who got their kicks in the counter-culture and social revolution); and with sneering disdain by those elites who look at the era as one of flaming excess and out-of-control gaudiness.

As I stated earlier, some labeled the era the Swinging Sixties. I guess that's because of the loose attitudes and morals that came forth in this decade; they didn't come up with the term "sex, drugs, and rock and roll" for nothing. The sex part I'll only touch on lightly; this is a family book, after all. But the drugs and the music? Yes, I'll be talking about those.

The years saw several "firsts." In 1960 the first televised debate for a presidential election was between Senator John F. Kennedy and Vice-President Richard M. Nixon. Nixon chose not to wear TV makeup, but Kennedy did, and it seemed to give him an edge. Also in the eyes of many Nixon appeared nervous, while Kennedy looked calmer. Although he was the first Roman Catholic to run for such a high office—and so inspiring not a little fear—Kennedy's success with the debate changed many people's minds about him.

This was the year NASA sent up ECHO, the first communications satellite to be seen with the naked eye … and believe me, my family and I went out to see it (although I never did). 1960 also saw an American "U2" spy plane shot down over the USSR. The capture of its pilot, Francis Gary Powers, riveted the country's attention, and was a real public relations coup for the Soviets.

The Olympic Games were held in Rome; there Wilma Rudolf, a black American woman, received three Olympic gold medals in track and field. The story is told of how, as a child, she was very ill with pneumonia and scarlet fever. She barely lived, and doctors said she probably would never walk again. But she never gave up hope, and was not only able to walk again, but able to outrun everyone else in the Olympics. And let's not forget about Cassius Clay, the boxer from Louisville, Kentucky who was later called Mohammed Ali. Years later, I remember how mad people got because he refused to fight in the war. I can still see the disgust in their faces. They thought he changed his name and religion because he was afraid of being shot. They also thought he was a big man in a ring with gloves on, but a coward when faced with a jungle and rifles and bombs and hand grenades.

In 1960 Elvis returned to the world's music scene after a two-year stint in the US Army, joining the other white male vocalists at the top of the charts: Bobby Darin, Neil Sedaka, Jerry Lee Lewis, Paul Anka, Del Shannon and Frankie Avalon.

America, however, was ready for a change; the Tamla Motown Record Company gave it to them. They came on the scene, specializing in black rhythm and blues, and aided in the emergence of female groups such as Gladys Knight and the Pips, Martha and the Vandellas, the Supremes, and Aretha Franklin. They also showcased some black men, including Smoky Robinson, James Brown, Jimi Hendrix, and the Temptations.

Bob Dylan helped bring about a folk music revival, along with Joan Baez and Peter, Paul & Mary. The Beach Boys began recording music that appealed to high schoolers. The Beatles, from England, burst into popularity with innovative rock music that seemed to speak to all ages. The Righteous Brothers were a popular white duo who used African-American styling to create a distinctive sound.

Television offered the second prime time cartoon show, the Flintstones, in 1960 (the first was Rocky and his Friends in 1959.) The show appealed to both children and adults, and set off a trend that included Alvin & the Chipmunks, the Jetsons, and Mr. Magoo. On the non-animated side, the Andy Griffith Show was the epitome of prime-time family television, and ran for most of the decade. Let me also touch on this, and I'll get into it more as we go along. Drug use was big coming into the Sixties, and only got bigger. Before it was over illegal narcotic use was so widespread that *Jefferson Airplane* co-founder Paul Kantner put it this way: "If you can remember anything about the Sixties, you weren't really there."

But the music was okay, some of it anyway. I'll be mentioning some of the acts that were approved by my parents for me to watch or listen to, and the ones that weren't. Most likely those won't surprise you, but you never know.

I know historians of all stripes have examined this rocky decade, picking and probing and pulling it apart like a frog in biology class. But I'm going to address these issues from another mindset, a mindset that hasn't been well served by these historians. Perhaps when I'm done you'll understand a bit more how much the incredible change this country went through in that turbulent decade is still having its way with us in this new, unsure millennium. They say the decade truly ended in 1973, I'm not going to speak much beyond 1969; things had pretty much calmed down by then.

So let's start with something most people can agree on: dogs.

We Texans love our dogs, and at three, I was no exception. Skippy, our red hound, was one terrific canine, the kind of dog every boy should have, and so rarely gets. And that dog could eat like nobody's business. My dad said you could clean the freezer out for him and Skippy would still be hungry. That gluttony caused him to come to a bad end. My mom and dad said one day he chased a rabbit and got lost and never found his way home. The truth of the matter was that daddy hauled him off; he had just gotten too expensive to keep, I guess.

I used to jump on Skippy and try to ride him, using his big long ears as reins. He would howl and walk around the porch of our unpainted clapboard house, but I don't think I was really hurting him. He was just doing what hound dogs do best. After a while he'd sit down until I lost interest and slid off his back.

One day Skippy ran off after my daddy, who was plowing a field near our house (Daddy was a farmer extraordinaire, and a wonderful man; I'll be speaking more of him and Momma and other people I knew as we go on). Being three, I followed him.

Some time later my mom noticed I was missing and went out on the porch to see where I was off to now (I always had the wander-bug; still do). Shielding her eyes from the bright Texas sun, she spotted the top of my head just over the terraces in the field where daddy was working, almost a quarter-mile away. She hopped in the car and started after me, I'm sure with her heart in her throat and blood in her eye.

When she apprehended me my only words I could say, babbled in my little, three-year-old voice were "My dog, my daddy." Obviously I was trying to explain the logic in following them both. I think she got it.

Another time my mom thought I'd run off (again), but I fooled her. I was asleep on the porch, hidden between Skippy's front and back legs. As mom opened the wooden screen door and approached us (I was told later), Skippy got up real gingerly, so as not to awaken me, and walked off. I slept on. Three-year-old Texas boys could sleep anywhere.

But Skippy had some competition, mainly from Smokey, our border collie. Momma frequently said you had to talk to Smokey like a human being because he was too smart to treat as a dog. Many times in the evening she or Daddy would step out on the porch and say, "Smokey, go get the cows." He'd amble off, and sometime later the cows would come home with the dog trotting along behind them (Daddy had trained him to do this, and Smokey loved showing off).

One hot July day they sent Smokey to get the cows. The cows came home but Smokey never did. We waited and waited, but that was it.

We think the neighbor might have had something to do with it (for some unfathomable reason he had it in for that dog), but we never found out. We didn't see any buzzards flying near where Smokey had gone—thinking maybe he'd broken a leg, or worse, and died where he fell—which led us to believe he'd been poisoned. (Buzzards will stay away from a poisoned carcass.) Maybe by that same neighbor (and I use the term advisedly). I never understood a few years later how a man who talked with such admiration of Willie Mays could not have liked Smokey.

I don't really believe in karma, but this neighbor's barn burned down a few years later. As I said, we never found out for sure what happened to that old dog.

Or for that matter, what happened to the neighbor's barn.

There were some pretty interesting things that happened in 1960. For one thing, technology was on the rise. The first working laser was demonstrated in May of that year at Hughes Research Laboratories. And how important did that turn out to be for us?

Plus for good or ill, the sexual revolution was upon us in full cry. With the availability of the pill people started having a freer attitude towards sex, along with a concurrent increase in unsafe sex. And we're still paying the freight for that today, what with AIDS and STDS and the whole alphabet soup of misery it brought us.

On the good side, Motown Records—which I already mentioned—was founded in 1960. Its first Top Ten hit was "Shop Around" by the Miracles in 1960 ... not that I was allowed to listen to it. The single peaked at number-two on the Billboard Hot 100, and was the company's first million-selling record. The Marvelettes then scored Motown Record Corporation's first US #1 pop hit, "Please Mr. Postman" in 1961. Motown would go on to score one hundred ten Billboard Top Ten hits during its run. The supergroup the Supremes alone scored twelve number one hit singles between 1964 and 1969, beginning with "Where Did Our Love Go."

But I'll talk more about world events, and how they affected us rural Texans, as we move on. Right now, I'd like to tell you a little bit about my ancestors. My mother is the great-granddaughter of a pioneer mentioned in some old family documents; he was my mother's father's grandfather.

This pioneer came to Texas from Mississippi to avoid the civil war when he was fifteen. There is a story that the slave woman who was his wet-nurse when he was a baby bawled and bawled the day he saddled up and rode off from his home.

His mother stayed up the night before baking biscuits. He came to Texas on horseback with a toe-sack full of those biscuits, and would hunt for meat as he traveled. In my mother's description of him, she mentions where he settled, Hamilton County. At some point in history, the county seat there allegedly had a racist billboard out on the edge of town, which was removed sometime in the Fifties. And no wonder. The message on that billboard had a warning that mentioned a racist word not used today followed by the phrase "don't let the sun set on your head." I don't believe my great-great grandfather pioneered that form of racism. My grandfather was named after him, but unfortunately most of his material riches were lost and were not passed down to him.

As a little boy of three, my grandparents held a special place of love in my heart. And they still do. My grandmother's maiden name was Kays, and they were "as poor as Job's turkey," as the country saying goes. I believe they may have been outcasts from their community. I don't know why I think that, it's just a feeling I have.

When I was growing up I would gaze at my great-grandparent's picture that hung on the wall in my grandparents' house and ask why they looked Japanese (dumb question). They weren't of course; they had Indian blood in their heritage. And what a heritage it was, living way back in the wild and wooly West. Just as a for instance, Great-Grandma Kays's mother went to school with Frank & Jesse James, and she and my great-grandma had experiences with Sam Bass (a famous local outlaw who terrorized the sleepy town of Round Rock, Texas).

My Grandma was a great one for stories, and to a little fella like me they were pure gold. Often times she'd tell tales that would start out something like this: "I was in town the other day and I met an old black lady walking on the sidewalk." (I don't remember my Grandma ever using the N-word) "She stopped me and said: *'I knows whose yous is. Yous looks jist lak Zack Kays. Yous must be hisn cuz yous look jist lak him.'*"

She never began a story like that, about white folk thinking she looked like her dad. Either the point of her anecdote was to laugh at how black people talked (which, knowing her, wasn't likely), or to illustrate how her family wasn't racist. Or it could have been a way for her to take pride in how she looked: Indian, like her father. Who knows, maybe it was all or none of the above.

But between the lines I see her telling a tale of an old cowboy who for some reason associated well with black folk. I'm talking about my great-grandpa, my mom's grandfather Zack. As I said, he was well accepted by the black community. That was a real accomplishment in those days, especially in that part of the country. But he came by that acceptance naturally. He was greatly influenced by a freed slave that helped raise him, a woman everybody called "Aunt Jennie." I wish I knew more about her.

But there was something very unusual about him.

Zack Kays was a "horse whisperer."

For those of you unfamiliar with the term, a horse whisperer is a person who has what seems an almost supernatural way with those animals. It's like they can understand each other, horse and human. And it's a gift, not something you can practice hard to achieve. Where I grew up, a real "horse whisperer" was a welcome sight to anyone who'd reached their wits' end with a cantankerous animal. The way it works looks deceptively easy. But only a person with that gift can really do it. Simply by stroking the horse's mane and whispering in its ear, such a person can calm a frightened or riled-up horse when literally nothing else can.

My grandma used to tell me stories how her daddy taught her how to ride a horse at a young age (she began riding when she was only four). In one of her tales she said that late one afternoon when she was around five years of age, she got on her horse to go find the cows.

On her way back home, the evening started coming on dark and oppressive. And that's when she began sensing something. As she risked a glance backward, her worst fears were confirmed. A pack of hungry wolves (she assured me they were not coyotes but I have no way of knowing) was shadowing her and the horse. She said the sound they made, howling in the woods, made her very afraid. She hoped things would work themselves out, but it wasn't to be. With a strangled scream and a whinny, the horse rose up and bolted like the devils of hell were on its tail. And as it ran, she found herself hanging on for dear life.

The animal jumped a creek, never breaking stride as it just kept running. Just as she was wondering how in the world she'd ever get the panicked creature to stop, it did, right in front of her house. All she had to do was climb down and hop on to the porch. The Horse Whisperer had trained the horse to bring his little girl to safety.

But it wasn't all sweetness and light. My Grandma was an inveterate worrier. She worried about little things and big, and did it all the time. For some reason, she seemed to have a lot of baggage in her life, and it plagued her health. Her constant fretting ended up giving her ulcers (I think she had seven stomach operations, but I only remember one of them). At any rate, I know she was sick a lot.

Grandma had an interesting way of talking. Usually she spoke just barely above a whisper, with her right pointer finger to her lip. And she was an outdoorswoman. She could identify nearly any tree just by looking at a piece of its bark or a leaf.

She really knew more about cows and horses and ranching than her husband Page ("Grandded", as I called him). In her day, she did a lot of plowing, but unlike most farm women, she wasn't a very good cook (I might as well be honest about that). In fact, my mom started cooking for the family at age fifteen. Now *she* was a good cook, although not as good a cook as my Mammaw (my dad's mom).

Both of my grandmothers were worry warts. Mammaw was a planner, and no matter how a plan went awry she would claim that it all worked out as she had thought; she merely had failed to tell *you* that she had changed the plan, and everything had gone just like she'd intended. Mom and I didn't believe her. I guess she really was good at coming up with a Plan B, or at least taking credit for a Plan B.

Mammaw really had a fear of crossing the old Ater Bridge. I don't know the origins of her fear of that bridge; it may have been the times that Pappaw slid his tractor down the bank and into the river. Mammaw never drove a car in her life (at least not from behind the steering wheel), although she was an excellent back seat driver. She provided directions and instructions all the time to anyone behind the wheel, especially Pappaw. People used to poke fun. "Poor old man, he couldn't drive if he didn't have his wife to tell him what to do." I'm not sure how bad a driver he actually was, but as I said, he did have a reputation for frequently putting his tractor in the river.

Getting back to the Ater Bridge, it was an iron framed old structure, with wooden planks. The planks were somewhat secured, creating a floor for a vehicle to drive over (provided it wasn't too big or heavy). The road came down a hill from the cemetery on the south side and narrowed as one crossed the bridge. On the north side of the bridge the road made an immediate ninety-degree turn to the east, and followed the river for a ways.

Mammaw lived in mortal fear of their car one day missing the bridge and crashing down the steep muddy banks, or falling to the water below. I couldn't blame her; it would have been at least a drop of twenty feet or so. Mammaw would holler to the driver to watch out, and then often times grab the door handle as though she was gonna jump out of the car as it was about to enter onto the bridge.

Sometimes her nerves would get the best of her and she would order the car be stopped before reaching the structure. She then would get out and walk across. Sounds safe enough at first blush, except for the fact that the old bridge had several large holes rotted away in the plank floor.

What complicated it even more was Mammaw was afraid to look down. She would begin her walk across that bridge with her head thrown all the way back, looking straight up. Then she would start singing a gospel hymn at the top of her lungs as her feet hit the part of the bridge that didn't have any ground underneath it.

I walked with her one time, and I have to admit those holes were big enough a person's leg could fall all the way through. I reckoned that a small boy like me might drop through completely. You'd look down at your feet and see the river flowing about twenty feet below. I warned her she needed to look down or she might fall through a hole and end up in the water below. She just kept on singing "Rock of Ages, cleft for me" and kept on walking with her nose to the sky. When she reached the other side, she climbed back in the car and we were on our way.

We all wondered how she would do after Pappaw died. How would a woman scared of her own shadow do after she lost her husband? It turned out the answer was, remarkably well. She was jolly and relaxed living in town. We figured a lot of her anxiety had been over Pappaw's poor health. Once he was gone most of her anxiety was gone too.
The exception was at Halloween. Mammaw was scared to death of trick or treaters, especially adolescents. She always came over and spent the night at our house then.

Grandded Page was very mechanically-minded, as well as being a good farmer. He loved to fish and play dominoes. He was well-known around town as a hard worker, but he also knew how to enjoy himself. One of the pictures I cherish is that of him and grandma getting their fishing tackle set up on the tailgate of their pickup, ready to wage war on the local Texas river-dwellers. They were clad in their usual duds, Grandma in a bonnet and Grandded in his battered cowboy hat. Truly, that was them in character and trust me, my Grandded was a character.

He had a rough start to his life. My Grandded's mom died when he was five, and when Page's dad remarried, he and his step mom didn't get along very well. Things came to head just three years later when she said, "he has got to go or I go." Bear in mind, Grandded was only eight years old at the time. So he left. After that he lived with various older brothers and sisters until he was thirteen, and then he was out on his own for good. He married Grandma when he was nineteen and she was a year younger.

My Grandded was probably the smartest man I ever knew or met, although the highest level he went to in school was third grade. He couldn't read, but he knew a lot; if pressed, he couldn't tell you how he knew it.

Everybody liked him, but he was extremely demanding on his family. I thought of him as my *On Golden Pond* grandfather who never thought anybody did anything right. You just couldn't win. Whatever you did, you could have done it better, or if you did it better, it was *"a waste of time, 'cause it wasn't somethin' you should have been doin' in the first place."* Not much encouragement from him, to say the least. He might brag all day about you to someone else, but he would never say it to your face.

Grandded cussed very frequently, but in some ways, it seems mild to the words uttered today, especially in many Rap songs. He smoked three packs of cigarettes a day, and smelled like it (but then everybody smelled like cigarettes, 'cause everyone smoked, or was a victim of secondhand smoke). Grandded also talked out loud in church, to our everlasting embarrassment. He loved to argue and he loved to talk politics.

When I was an adult, about a week or two before he died I asked him if he had any regrets. He only said, *"I wished somebody had kept my back end in school so I could have amounted to somethin'."* When he told me that, I frowned, assuring him he had amounted to a lot. He just shook that off. And then he said something strange: *"I coulda bought a blackland farm with the money I spent on doctors for Grandma."* Pretty rough, huh?

I think he had a chip on his shoulder. He felt compelled to constantly prove he knew more than others: him, the grandson of one of the richest men in Hamilton County, and then left on his own, uneducated and with no inheritance. His brothers and sisters called him Casey even though his first and middle name was Page Meredith (the original "Boy Named Sue", a Johnny Cash song). And I think having to endure that handle all his life is part of what made him as tough as a boot. Later I found out the meaning of the word "Casey" is brave, so his brothers and sisters must have seen that in him.

I liked that. I liked it so much I named my second son Joshua Casey. The rest of the world may call my son Joshua, but his family will always call him Casey, after my Grandfather, a brave and smart man.

My other grandfather (I called him Pappaw)—my dad's dad—was a kind and gentle man. He was a perfectionist, and was known to plow up a perfectly good stand of a crop because he wasn't satisfied with it. Then he would replant and ultimately get a thicker stand that he was more satisfied with.

My Pappaw teased me a lot before my sister was born. So much so, it irritated my mom a little. He was really a sweet old man, but he kept telling me that I was gonna get a "black baby" (only, he didn't use the word "black". He didn't mean anything bad by this; it was just the way he and others talked). Sure, it was wrong, but it was a hold over phrase from another era. If you didn't live back then, you may never understand that there were different levels of animosity. My Pappaw's level of animus towards another race was almost nonexistent. When my sister was born she was really red from crying, and she had long fingernails which she kept scratching herself with and aggravating the skin color.

I was only four when I saw her for the first time. Looking up at Pappaw I said, "Well, she may be black, but we're gonna keep her anyway."

He was much older than my mom's dad, and owned outright one hundred acres of land. Fifty acres were on the Leon River bottom at Ater, Texas (another wide spot in the road in Coryell County).

He was of German heritage and had a speech impediment. Some claimed they could barely understand him due to his German accent, but in reality, it was his impediment that threw them off. In 1912, when he was twelve years old, he'd walked to Texas alongside a covered wagon from Arkansas, with his parents and others.

His name was Rupert and he had a twin named Robert. They had other brothers and sisters, most notably another brother named Ruel. Rupert, Robert and Ruel all raised their families near the Leon River at Ater. Although they were much more established, they had little more during the Great Depression than my mom's parents had. They taught my father well.

My dad Charles was born in 1933, in a house near Arnett, Texas. He went to school in Jonesboro Texas, and at some point, lived in the Ater community. He helped his dad build their house there, and is buried in the Ater Cemetery along with most of my relatives.

My dad was a man who was also tough and hardworking. Here was a guy who had nothing but sweat equity to put on the table. My mom said he taught her how to take care of money. He'd often tell her, "Don't worry about sales and bargains, Jo Dean; there will always be one when you got the money." The Whisenhunts didn't—and still don't—believe in borrowing money (in theory).

Instead of him putting money in the bank for me, one time he bought some kid goats and rigged up a board with holes and rubber straps that allowed him to bottle feed all of them at the same time. When they were old enough to sell, he used the money to buy me a savings bond. And that's just how he did things. He might not have enough money to buy the bond itself, but he'd work it to have enough money to buy a calf or goat. Then he would raise it until he could sell it for enough to buy one.

I often envision him in his typical work attire, which were a khaki shirt and a pair of blue jeans. Many times he didn't wear a hat. Sometimes he'd abandon the cowboy boots for lace up work ones. Unlike my mother's father, who had work time and play time, my dad's work *was* his play time. He might stop in the middle of something and talk to a neighbor for three hours, but he never intentionally sought out entertainment. Whenever daddy wasn't eating or sleeping or reading his Bible, he was working. If he couldn't get in to a field due to bad weather or it was too muddy, he was toiling away on a piece of equipment so it would be ready when he needed it. The only time we ever went to visit somebody was either on a Sunday, or when it rained and he was caught up on his equipment repairs. To this day, when it rains I get the urge to go somewhere. Otherwise I prefer to stay home and work on my place.

I lovingly recall my daddy's red arms and red neck ... not a Jeff Foxworthy comic character, but an integral piece of humanity: the plain, unassuming hard-working American. Not looking for much—if anything—from anyone. Simply a hard and good man just trying to carve out his place in the sun ... and "kissed" by that sun on the skin that was left exposed. My dad was the youngest of five children, and his oldest brother was sixteen years older than him. He only had one sister, who was the next to the youngest (she was five years older than him).

Years later at his funeral all my childhood people came up and told me how good a man my father was. They all talked about how few words he spoke, and about how hard he worked and how honest he was. They went on to say he was one of the toughest men they ever knew, and never backed down from anything. And that's true, he didn't.

When Daddy was alive there were several times when he'd be called to come over to someone's house because there was a state boy outside who wandered off from the grounds (a state boy was one incarcerated in the Texas Juvenile Detention Center, not far from where we lived). It was usually some woman whose husband was in town and could not be reached. (Remember, no one had a cell phone.)

My daddy never took a weapon, or seemed the least bit scared. There were times I saw him walk up to one of these adolescents, and they would just start talking. Eventually the state guards would show up and they would drive off with the boy. I never knew what was said. I just remember seeing him and the boy setting on a porch step talking.

I don't have many stories about Uncles Lawrence, Harold, Troy and Aunt Ruberta. My Mammaw was an excellent cook, and since Lawrence, Harold and Ruberta lived several hours away, we would have quite a feast when any of them came back for a visit. Mammaw cooked for the Jonesboro Public School for sixteen years. The school superintendent let her plan and buy all the food, as well as cook it. Rest assured this was not normal school slop; everybody loved her cooking. My dad said the kids could go back through the line and get seconds (and they did)!

As an aside, to this day my favorite foods are simple country fare: round steak for dinner (what other people call lunch), and round steak for supper, which is, well, *supper*. In the Sixties we had not heard of pizza, and the only Mexican food we knew of was tamales. The only fast food restaurants were Dairy-Queen and A&W, or a knock off of A&W.

My mom was the youngest of four kids, all born and raised through the Great Depression. Her brother Uncle Ray and sister Aunt Berta Mae were the oldest, and twins. They were born prematurely, and at birth each one was so small they fit in a cigar box. The doctor said they wouldn't live, and just laid them on the bed while he worked on Grandma to save her life. Great-Grandma and Great-Grandpa Kays picked them up and held them over the top of the wood stove, gently massaging the infants while doctor desperately did his job. And it must have worked: mother and babies all lived and thrived. Mom's other brother, Uncle Dale, was a colorful character. He was impetuous, like his older sister Berta Mae. They seemed more like twins than Ray and Berta Mae.

The year my mom was born was 1937, right in the heart of the Great Depression. Mom was the valedictorian of her class, but it was a little one; I think they had less than ten kids in her senior class. On the other hand, Daddy was a C student (there were about the same number of kids in his graduating class as well).

Mom was a great cook, serving fried round steak, milk gravy, fried okra, and light bread for sopping gravy. My mother's tea was a dessert in itself, almost as sweet as watermelon juice. As a kid, a true dessert would be watermelon and home-made ice cream. My mom could make pies pretty enough to be in a magazine. They tasted good too. Her most famous was lemon chess, but my favorites were coconut cream and chocolate cream.

Growing up I heard a lot of Depression stories, and they've made me very grateful for the blessings my family and I enjoy today. Some of the best were what we Texans call "boll pull stories." For those who don't know what a boll pull is (and I'd bet that's most of you), the term has to do with harvesting cotton (the "boll"). Somebody told me there's a difference between pickin' cotton and pullin' cotton, but I can't remember what it is … even though I was told several times.

My mom and her family would miss the first six weeks of school every year because they would be out in West Texas on a boll pull. And the places they stayed while they did this each had their own stories. Once they lived in a brand-new barn that hadn't been used yet. Another time they stayed in an old house that had wallpaper draped across overhead to create a ceiling.

And this was a real place to remember.

One night just as supper began, a snake crawled unseen off the rafter and onto the wallpaper "ceiling." His weight caused the paper to tear, and he fell right on the kitchen table. I imagine that was it for supper that night.

Over the years I heard a lot of good-natured ribbing between my mom and her siblings about who worked the most and who worked the least in those cotton patches. Allegedly Dale and Berta Mae goofed off a lot, but Dale could actually pick or pull more when he set his mind to it. Usually he paid a price for that, as his sack would also have more sticks and rocks than others. My mom claimed her Daddy said her sack always had the cleanest cotton.

Lots of times Berta Mae might be found without her sack, investigating various holes she found. Once she discovered a momma skunk and a bunch of babies. She and Dale were able to get the babies out of the hole without getting sprayed ... which is a neat trick in itself. Dale and Berta Mae always seemed to live charmed lives, abiding right on the edge, and living to tell about it. The cautious ones were Uncle Ray and my mom.

And that seemed to hold mom in good stead, especially when it came to raising me.

CHAPTER 2

◆

1961

And now I was four, and quickly becoming a fan of television. I liked all kinds of shows: *The Beverly Hillbillies, Rifleman, Rawhide, Cheyenne, Laramie, Huckleberry Hound, Pixie and Dixie, Top Cat, Popeye, Merry Melodies, Captain Kangaroo, Mr. Peppermint,* and *Slam Bang Theatre.*

The supernatural and science fiction blended in many of the popular shows of the Sixties, including *Bewitched, The Addams Family, My Favorite Martian, I Dream of Jeannie, Star Trek, The Outer Limits,* and *Twilight Zone.* Also in the late 60's, irreverent humor from vaudeville days was revived in a show called *Rowan and Martin's Laugh-In,* where many regular performers and guests became part of a show biz classic.

Do you remember the TV show *Have Gun Will Travel*? It was a Western, and the main character, a gunslinger that only went by the name Paladin, handed out business cards containing the show's title. I loved it. Paladin just plain old *looked* dangerous. He carried a derringer as well as matching pistols, and sported a big black hat and mustache. At the stores, they sold a Paladin toy set with all the gear (including the mustache and hat). I only remember going to the movies once, and it was to see *Born Free*. Years later I saw *Batman* at a drive-in.

I guess you couldn't blame me for liking television so much. TV brought the world and all its charms—and depredations—to us simple country folks in rural Texas. And we'd never be the same.

One of the earliest shows I remember was *Pete and Gladys*. The show was a situation comedy broadcast by CBS on Monday night at 8:00 PM. It ran for two seasons, beginning September 19, 1960. The last episode aired on September 10, 1962. Character actor Harry Morgan—who would find real fame years later when he played Colonel Sherman T. Potter on *M*A*S*H*—was Pete. His wife Gladys was played by Cara Williams, who bore an uncanny resemblance to Lucille Ball; they could have been sisters.   During this broadcast every Monday night, Harry Morgan, while in character as Pete (and he'd always be Pete, to me anyway) would plug Carnation Milk. He pitched its smoothness, creaminess, and all-around goodness. That was all it took. If Pete said it was great stuff, that was okay in my book. I started begging my mom to buy it. Matter of fact, I didn't leave her alone about it.

One Saturday morning, she'd had it. While at the store she finally gave in and bought me a can (knowing full well what would happen next). When she got home she showed me the can, took the opener, opened the stuff front of me, and poured it in a glass. Eagerly I picked up the glass and took a pull, anticipating the most wonderful taste bud experience. Not hardly. Plainly put, it was the worst thing I'd ever had in my mouth. Spitting it back into the glass I exclaimed, "But Pete said it was good!"

My mother's reply was well-earned smugness "You've learned a valuable lesson; you can't believe everything you see on TV."

I can contrast this experience with the milk I usually drank, from our own cows. Now that was good stuff, but there is a certain way you have to process raw milk to make it drinkable. I recall watching my parents not only milk the cows, but then bring the milk in the house and pour it through a cloth before placing it in the refrigerator (we called it an ice box then, even though it was really a refrigerator; our radio sat on top). We only bought pasteurized milk from the grocery store in the spring, because that's when the cow would eat too many wild onions and other weeds, making the milk taste funny.

Getting back to TV. Another show we'd watch pretty regularly was *Naked City*. It was a police drama, and it had two different runs, between 1958 and 1963. Lots of critics say it was one of television's most innovative police shows, and one of its most important and influential drama series. I guess it was more character anthology than police procedural. The show blended the grittiness of *Dragnet* with the urban pathos of the Studio One school of TV drama, offering a mix of action-adventure and grim sets, car chases and character studies, shoot-outs and sociology, all filmed with arresting starkness on the streets of New York.

But … there was that show's crazy title to get past: *Naked City*. One night I remember my mom becoming extremely exasperated with me, and it had to do with my pronunciation of this show (and not just because I couldn't pronounce the letter *L* until halfway through first grade). Maybe the true story of the program's demise is because all throughout the country, parents were having similar conversations with their kids.

The show's signature was its narrator, who introduced each episode with the sonorous assurance that the series was not filmed in a studio, but "in the streets and buildings of New York itself." To us that was heady stuff. The narrator then returned thirty minutes later to intone the series' famous tag-line (also borrowed from the feature): "There are eight million stories in the Naked City. This has been one of them." What wasn't to like?

Well, as I said, the show's title for one thing. To me, even at four it sounded faintly racy, and I just couldn't seem to get my head around the name. I remember trying to get my parents help to figure it out. As near as I can recall, this is how it went. "Momma, what is a neck-ed city?" I asked, looking up at her (regardless of my slight speech impediment, people say I talked well for my age).

"It's a story about New York City."

"Then why do they call it neck-ed?"

She didn't answer right away. "I don't know, they just do," my mom finally replied.

I couldn't let it go. "So what does neck-ed mean?"

She blew out a breath. "It's not neck-ed, it's nake-ed."

I tried it. "Neck …ed."

"Nake-ed," my mom said.

"Neck …ed."

By now Dad was really becoming exasperated. "*Nake*-ed!" he called out.

I scrunched up my nose. "Neck …ed."

Mom's face grew red. I could tell she and my Dad were growing irritated as I talked while they were trying to listen to the program. "Nake-ed. You're saying the word wrong. The word is NAKE …ED."

There was another pause, and then I said, "Well, what does neck-ed *mean?*"

"It means not wearing clothes," mom said, "but the show is called Nake-ED City."

That brought up a new thought. "So how come they got all their clothes on?"
Dad shot me a look. "Would you be quiet so we can hear the TV?"

"Is the policeman after that guy because he took his clothes off?" I asked.

"No!" mom yelled.

"So where are the people that don't got any clothes on?"

"There *ain't* anybody that took their clothes off," Mom said. "It's a show about some policeman in New York City and everybody has their clothes on."

"Well, is that neck-ed city close to New York City?"

Mom just stared at me. "No, it's the same place and they all have their clothes on and it's called NAKE. ED. *CITY !!!*"

After another very long pause, and assuming that neck-ed must mean no clothes and naked must mean something else (but still not being able to pronounce *nake*), I said, "What does that word you're saying mean?"

"What word?" Mom asked.

"The word that that city is."

"Naked?"

"Yes."

My Dad chimed in, "Naked mean no clothes on but this is a story of New York and they're trying to say it's more like the real way policemen and bad guys act."

"Neck-ed and neck-ed are the same word?"

"There's only one word," Mom said, "and it's *naked* and you're calling it neck ed."

"Well, why do they want to call it that word if they all have their clothes on?"   By this point my parents were done talking, tuning me out and becoming fully engulfed in the stupid show with the stupid name.

That was it. I walked into another room to find something else to do. I think maybe I was more exasperated than my parents. It wasn't *my* fault they didn't know what I was talking about.

Many years later Buck Owens would sing, "I wouldn't live in New York City if they gave me the whole town." I couldn't blame him. It surely had something to do with it being a neck-ed city.

There was another TV show called *It's a Man's World,* which the Internet says lasted only one season. I remember a conversation about that show, with more confusion. I don't think I was as at wit's end with its premise, but my mother probably was. Other than the title, I don't recall it as clearly as *Naked City.*

The conversation revolved around dialogue I had with Dad about what a world was. I apparently asked what a world was and they explained that it was the earth. Then they had to explain it was dirt … I definitely remember something about it being dirt. Then there was some discussion about God making the dirt, so how could it be a man's world? Even then somehow, I'd grasped the fact that earth was made of dirt. Of course, since God made the dirt, I reasoned the *world* was more of how it operated; not a bad leap for a four-year-old boy. I don't remember how Mom and Dad explained it but somehow, I got it.

Then I remember asking if men really did get to be in charge of the operations. That was all it took.

I distinctly recall my Dad saying yes. That made me glad, since that meant I was a *de facto* member of the winning gender. My mom grew very silent, but didn't disagree. I then asked her, since she was really on the losing side, I guess that meant she wasn't really in charge of anything. Basically, she answered in the affirmative, but her voice was soft. I don't think she was mad. More as if she was… resigned, somehow. Looking back on it, I suppose Mom understood women can influence men quite well, so there wasn't any need to be "in charge." I don't remember anything much else, save for the fact she assured me I did *not* outrank her, in spite of my gender. The least vague things about that conversation were: 1) Dad having said yes, men were in charge, and 2) my being glad that some day I'd get to be in charge.

As for as the show, it seemed to me like the men on it weren't really in charge of anything. I don't think it held my interest.

But I wasn't alone in my quest for knowledge. In the glow of television screens all across America children were trying to come to grips with how the world worked, whether they were watching this show or something else.

Generations earlier, in the glow of countless campfires, children across America (and doubtless throughout the earth) had tried to understand how the world and its ways worked, entranced by tales of the Storytellers. These were men and women who seemed to have a natural, intuitive grasp of things, and could transmit those truths to others in ways anybody could understand.

I can only imagine how a Storyteller would link some nugget of knowledge to a particular night sky, or perhaps to a certain campsite, or maybe to even a flicker of a flame. Apparently as a child in the Sixties I have linked some nuggets to a flicker from an electron gun, and a glass tube coated with phosphor. It doesn't sound very wholesome when I put it that way, does it? Only one generation prior, people had been taught and entertained by sound coming through a cloth-covered speaker, but my generation had sound and sight bombarding us; a family gathering around a campfire that *talked* to us.   But that's enough heavy philosophy for now. Because another neat thing about 1961 was my little sister Darla coming to us in November of that year, close to my fourth birthday. She was our treasure, that's what we called her, and the first time I saw her I didn't think I'd ever seen anything prettier. Somewhere there's a photo of me wearing an Indian headdress, whooping a war dance next to her basinet. Even at that young age I was determined to protect her any way I could.

And speaking of protection, there's another thing I need to mention about 1961, and it pertains to my dad. For a few days in late March he seemed more nervous than usual, constantly asking mommy if a certain document had come. Every day he seemed to be unusually interested in the mail. The news on the radio seemed to capture his attention as well. Neighbors tried to comfort him, but daddy seemed restless.

Then one day something came: a letter. After tearing it open and reading it, Daddy's whole demeanor changed. He stopped everything and went straight to town and bought a frame. He came home and found a nail and put the paper he received into the frame and put it on the wall. He seemed proud, but mostly relieved.

I asked mommy what this all meant and she said it meant Daddy would not have to go to Cuba. Mommy told me that Mr. Kennedy was fixin' to make the army go fight some bad people down in Cuba, but that paper Daddy had just got meant that he wouldn't have to go.

What Daddy had gotten in the mail was an honorary discharge, because he went to Greenland when we were fighting the Koreans. Later I found out that afterward he'd gone into the reserves and attended school on the GI Bill, but hadn't actually received his discharge papers until that day in 1961. By then President Kennedy had frozen all the discharges, and that's why daddy was so worried, thinking he might be called back. But daddy got his before the freeze.

Mommy said while he was in the service he drove a truck and the weather was really cold, but he didn't have to fight anybody because there weren't any Koreans in Greenland. Every time mom or I talked about Greenland, Daddy would correct us and say it was "Baffin Bay, not Greenland." Mom would say that Baffin Bay was part of Greenland; daddy would mutter that it wasn't.

One time I asked why they sent Daddy to Greenland if there weren't any Koreans to fight. Mommy said he was there to keep the Russians away … and I had no idea who they were. All I know was a discharge meant you didn't have to fight no more and that "honorary" meant that Daddy had done really good when he was in the army. My dad never seemed very boastful and I know he knew he'd already done good.

The paper on the wall was to show the army that he and them were done for good and all, if they ever decided to come over to the house to make him fight again. Anyway, that Honorary Discharge hung on his bedroom wall above the butane heater for the rest of his life.

I later noticed when we went to other people's houses they had papers like that hung on their walls too. Everybody thought that paper was important. Most everybody had pictures on their wall, but this paper had no picture.

It was important just the same.

Another one of my earliest memories is the church we attended from 1957 until 1967, Stanley Chapel. The church was further away from the house than the lost ninety (the acreage my daddy farmed); I understand it has since been converted into a house.

It'd only had indoor plumbing for a short time when I found a snake drinking from the commode; I'll talk more about our Texas snakes later.

The members of this church were our neighbors and relatives. I used to stand on the porch and shake everybody's hand as they entered. People used to say I was gonna grow up to be a preacher or a politician 'cause of the way I shook everyone's hand. And that was okay to me. Even at that young age I thought about God a lot. Many times, I would lie on the ground, just looking up at the sky. It always made me feel closer to Him. From the farm to the church, there was a creek that had to be crossed. Occasionally I would get dirty between the time I was dressed for church and the time we got there. Sometimes we would stop at Dodd's Creek for one last face washin'. By the way, as kids we drank from this creek from time to time, and the water was delicious.

On the side of the building we'd catch lightning bugs, and rub the bug juice on our arms; it made for a pretty eerie sight on a hot August night, watching kids run around in the dark with their arms glowing green. The church had been constructed by flagstones and had a small grove of cedars on the east side that contained a sticky wax coating. If you rubbed against the trunks of them, you'd get that sticky wax on you. You can imagine me coming home from church with cedar wax on me and lightning bugs squished on my arms. To my thinking, if you weren't getting dirty you weren't having fun.

Something else happened in 1961 which would affect not only America, but the entire world for the next decade and beyond: The Soviet Union and the United States had gotten involved in the space race. As my Daddy explained, they were trying to see who could get a man in space first. The idea was that whichever country did this would control the "high ground" of the heavens, and thus rule the world. I know that to modern ears this sounds ludicrous, but remember the Cold War was still in full swing, and been since the late forties; in those days paranoia was the way of things. This race led to an increase in spending on science and technology, a lot of which we're still enjoying.

But for America, it appeared we'd lost that race when on April 12, 1961, the Soviets beat us to the punch, and sent cosmonaut Yuri Gagarin into orbit around the Earth in a capsule called Vostok 1.

That was it. You would have thought Armageddon had hit.

The country went into an absolute panic mode, including us down in Texas. In response President John F. Kennedy, who along with Vice-President Lyndon Johnson had taken office that same year, pulled out all the stops. He'd already given his famous speech which included the immortal words, "Ask not what your country can do for you, but what you can do for your country." Now it was time to step up to the plate.

And we did. The National Aeronautics and Space Administration—NASA—was born, and the nation went into an all-out mode not seen since World War II. A year earlier, in 1960, the United States had sent up ECHO, the first communications satellite seen with the naked eye. That was good, but it wasn't enough. The Soviets had now sent the first man into space and the Americans needed a man in space, too.

We accomplished that when less than three weeks later, on May 5, 1961, Alan Shepard rode his Redstone rocket into space, and history, in the *Freedom 7*. Just a couple of weeks after that, on May 25, President Kennedy said he wanted to have a man on the moon and back before the decade was over. He announced Project Apollo, vowing we'd be first there, and before the 1960s was over. It was a pretty gutsy thing to promise, but we did that too. America won the race hands down when it placed the first men on the moon, astronauts Neil Armstrong and Buzz Aldrin, in July 1969.

By 1961 popular music was changing too, into an era of "all hits", as numerous artists released recordings. The early developments of the Motown Sound, folk rock, and the beginning of the "British Invasion" of bands from the U.K all whetted the appetites of American youth. The invasion consisted of bands such as the Beatles, the Dave Clark Five, the Rolling Stones, and others, and are major examples of American listeners expanding from the folksinger sounds of the 1950s and evolving into new types of music. But the year also saw the dark beginnings of a war which would eventually tear the country apart. The start of it was simple enough, when President Kennedy sent a group of people to Vietnam to report the conditions, along with approximately seven hundred of our American forces. But I guess the trouble had really started when the people of North Vietnam decided to take over South Vietnam. The South Vietnamese people didn't want that, so they tried to fight back. Soon the Americans pushed their way in the war. They thought that if South Vietnam didn't want to be part of North Vietnam, they shouldn't be bossed around. And so, America began to fight for South Vietnam.

A report known as the "December 1961 White Paper" was generated, arguing for more military and economic aid there. It also called for the introduction of a large-scale number of American "advisers" to help stabilize the Diem regime and pound the NLF, the National Liberation Front. That began a conflict which wouldn't see an end until some fourteen years later, in 1975.

The Counterculture Revolution was cranking up in 1961, and had a big effect on cinema. This was the beginning of the New Hollywood era, a mindset that would dominate the next decade in theatres and revolutionized the movie industry.

Popular music showcased an era of "all hits" as numerous artists had released recordings beginning in the 1950s as 45-rpm "singles" (one-song records with another song on the flip side); radio stations tended to play only the most popular of the wide variety of records being made. Also, bands tended to record only the best of their songs as a chance to become a hit record.

The rise of the counterculture, particularly among the youth, created a huge market for rock, soul, pop and blues music produced by the drug-culture. This was influenced by bands such as The Doors, The Rolling Stones, Led Zeppelin, Cream, The Grateful Dead, Jefferson Airplane, Janis Joplin, The Who, Sly and the Family Stone, The Jimi Hendrix Experience, The Incredible String Band, and others. Radical music in the folk tradition was pioneered by the likes of Bob Dylan, The Mamas and the Papas, and Joan Baez in the United States, and in England, by the single name performer Donovan.

Radio continued to be the primary means of listening to music, with the major development being a change from primarily AM to FM. This gave a much purer, clearer signal … needed for the music that was to come. Radio was supplemented by music on TV, which showcased *American Bandstand*.

An hour-long dance party program hosted by the ageless Dick Clark, *AM*, as it was called, was watched by teens from coast to coast. From it they not only learned the latest music, but how to dance to it. When Chubby Checker introduced the Twist on the show in 1961, a new craze was born, and dancing became an individual activity—which to us made no sense at all. A lot of people thought it became so popular because it helped them let go of the Cold War tension. To me that sounds like a bunch of psycho-babble mumbo-jumbo, but who knows.

The Mashed Potato, the Swim, the Watusi, the Monkey and the Jerk followed up, all mimicking their namesakes. Each new dance often lasted for just a song or two before the next hot thing came along. As the Sixties went on eventually the names and stylized mimicry of the dances ceased and the dancers just moved however they wanted. For those who preferred *watching* the dancers, the industry gave them go-go girls, nubile young women up on stages in large "bird cages," who gyrated above the crowd.

Of course, we Texans just all thought they were nuts.

CHAPTER 3

1962

This was the year that things changed dramatically in the United States, but nobody really knew it then. It happened when the Supreme Court decided in *Engel v. Vitale* (court docket 370 U.S. 421, 1962, if you care) that prayer in the public schools was declared unconstitutional. We wouldn't know for years yet how far-reaching that decision would be, but a lot of people can point to that ruling as the day things started turning sour for our country.

In the Sixties people also started becoming more concerned with their health and the environment, and we're still seeing this today. In addition, consumer advocate Ralph Nader wrote a book called *Unsafe at Any Speed,* which addressed safety concerns with the auto industry in general, and with the Chevy Corvair in particular. This in turn led to the birth of the consumer movement.

And speaking of birth (and the lack thereof), the year 1967 saw birth control pills becoming common; along that line, that same year saw Colorado become the first state (of many) to legalize abortion. We're still paying for that today as well.

Also in 1962 Rachel Carson, a scientist and writer, warned that our earth would die of pollution and chemicals, especially chemicals that were developed to kill harmful insects, if we didn't take steps to stop it.

DDT was considered the worst of these. It killed everything, bad insects along with the good, not to mention many plants and animals. She wrote the book *Silent Spring* with this dire warning. In response, at least five states banned the chemical. The book also fanned the environmental movement, and the Sierra Club gained a following.

The space race was heating up on all fronts as well. The following year, 1963, during a five-hour flight astronaut John Glenn became the first man to orbit the earth three times. America went crazy over him.

A year before, in 1961, something else important happened, and it likewise started out seemingly small. Here's what it was. Soon after overtaking Cuba Fidel Castro declared that he was a communist, and the United States broke off diplomatic relations.

In response Castro seized American property down there. The CIA attacked Cuba in an ill-fated mission at the Bay of Pigs (earlier that year one of our U-2 spy planes had identified long range missiles parked there). President John F. Kennedy readied troops to invade Cuba, and the Soviet Union prepared to fire at US cities if we made a move. It was a tense time for everybody, but luckily the Russians blinked first. I don't think anybody but a select few knew how close we'd come to worldwide thermonuclear war.

Of course, at age five I had no idea of any of this. Truth be told, little boys of five are notoriously cavalier about many things—including body functions—and I was no exception. I peed off the front porch a lot, but only remember getting in trouble for it when company was over (it might be that was the only time I got caught). Of course, we had no bathroom in the house. We had an outhouse, and it wasn't for taking a bath; we did that in a number three wash tub on the back porch except in the winter. In the winter, the wash tub was placed in the kitchen.

Anyway, for me the outhouse was only for really important business (if you know what I mean). Outhouses are pretty intimidating, especially when you're a small child. It's a wonder any of us got potty trained. Can you imagine today if every time our children went to the bathroom, we had to remind them to watch out for snakes? You had to fear the rebuke from your parents more than the fear of being snake bit before you were ever fully potty trained in those days. (I know that the origin of some of my low self-esteem issues occurred in our backyard between the house and the outhouse and being called a "sissy" when I was only a three and four-year old.)

However, I don't remember actually ever seeing a snake in an outhouse. On the contrary, I'll never forget when the small country church we attended got an indoor toilet. One hot summer day, right as services were over, I stepped inside the john. Just as I was unzipping my pants—or breeches as I used to call them—much to my surprise I saw a large snake draped over the toilet seat, getting a drink from the bowl. The small brown flagstone building had no air conditioning, and no screens on the doors. I suppose the snake had crawled inside and into the toilet for a cool refreshing drink.

I remember the old outhouse there. It always had a strong odor and was at least a two-holer. The church had a capped well in the front yard, and the hitching posts were still standing from an earlier era when people rode to church on horseback, or arrived by horse and carriage. The large stinky structure was across the dirt road that ran north and south along the west side of the church, and was positioned on the northwest side of the church. It was a long walk to it, and as I said it smelled bad, and you had to really want to go in order to make the trek.

We did not move into a house with an indoor toilet until much later in my fifth year. In fact, we moved on my birthday, November 23rd, 1962. My sixth birthday was quite memorable as well, but that's a story for the next chapter.

Our first indoor toilet had a bathtub with feet. It looked similar to those bath tubs you'd see in the western movies. Indoor bathrooms back then smelled different, not only different from outhouses but different from today's bathrooms. Back then the hot water heater was free-standing somewhere in the same room. The caution changed from "watch out for snakes" (the usual outhouse warning), to "don't slam the door." Because if you slammed the door, you could easily blow out the pilot light on the water heater. And then the gas would overtake you. And then you'd die. Or the house might fill with gas and then Dad might come home smoking a cigarette and blow the house up. Can you tell I came from a long line of worry warts? Often you could smell the butane in the bathrooms, even when the pilot was lit.

But getting back to outhouses and their charms, my grandparents had one with a warped door that didn't close well. Oftentimes, since the door didn't stay closed unless it was locked from the inside, chickens would linger around inside the outhouse. Why they did, was anybody's guess; I sure wouldn't have. I know on a hot summer day it was best to get your business done inside there as quickly as possible, and then move on.

It became second-nature to always open the door wide, and then to step out of the way to let the chickens clear out before going in to take care of things. I remember one time we were visiting at my grandparents, and all my cousins were there. We kids were running and playing like a bunch of wild Indians (a figure of speech, we weren't actually playing that we were Indians, but many times we did), and having great fun.

On this occasion, I was walking through the house, taking a break from whatever it was that I was doing … probably looking to see if dinner was ready. As an aside, I've mentioned that dinner in those days is what we call lunch today. Back then, it was breakfast, dinner and supper, not breakfast, lunch and dinner. Confusing, huh?

Anyway, while strolling through the house I got nature's call and started rapidly for the outhouse. Instead of the usual snake warning, my mom reminded me about the chickens. My reply was a quick, "I know," as I raced out the back door.

As anticipated, several dim-witted chickens raced around and scurried about when I opened the door that was ajar. I even had to scare a couple more out once I was inside. The next step was to secure the door well; there were cousins aplenty running and playing all over the yard, and I was modest enough to not want any embarrassing situations to take place if the door wasn't shut properly. Once it was secure, I quickly and efficiently dropped my breeches down around my ankles, all the while backing up toward the wooden bench with the round, cut-out hole.

Just as I began to sit down, a chicken hen came flying out of that hole as if it had been launched off the flight deck of an aircraft carrier. I almost had an accident right then, and rushed like a wild man to get out of the way.

Now we had quite a predicament going on. I had a crazy, terrified hen fluttering about at my ankles, growing even more frightened and hysterical each time I leaned down to pull my pants up. I'd go one way, and she'd pick that exact moment to go the same way, almost like she was trying to cut me off.

This went on for a very long time. Finally, I scared the chicken close enough to the door that I could pull my breeches up to my knees without getting a face full of feathers. But now the really hard part was coming up: how to get the door open and get the chicken out without exposing myself to any of my girl cousins, who were even then circling the house and passing within view on a regular basis.

Trying to listen over the frantic cackling of the nearly out-of-its-mind hen, I finally caught a break when I heard my cousins' laughter fading as they made their exit from the back yard to the front. They were completely oblivious of the turmoil going on inside the outhouse. This was my chance. Quickly I got the door open and shooed the chicken out, managing to get the door closed before my cousins made another re-entry in to the back yard.

After I finally got to sit down, I realized I no longer had the urge to do the business I'd intended to do. It was as gone as yesterday's dreams. Thoroughly wiped out (so to speak), I went back in the house to wash for dinner.

Just as my mom began to ask if I'd washed, she must have realized I'd returned from the facility sooner than expected. When she stated, "I thought you had to go to the outhouse," I simply replied, "I decided I didn't need to go", never mentioning anything about the event that had just transpired. It seemed to have lasted for an eternity, but had only been less than a few minutes.

Even though I had my problems with chickens, generally I like animals. Especially dogs. Earlier in this book I mentioned the dogs we had when I was very small, Smokey and Skippy. After they were gone, one day when I was five I remember going to Mammaw and Pappaw's house. For some reason, my parents were not with me.

But that was okay, because Pappaw had a surprise for me. He took me down the road from his house to his neighbor, Jeff Buckner's house. When we got there Jeff led us to his garage, and opened the door. My eyes bugged out as a grin split my face. There were a whole bunch of Border collie puppies frolicking in there on the floor, and they all started barking to raise the roof when Jeff opened the garage door.

Looking down, Pappaw asked me which one I wanted. But although I was thrilled, I couldn't decide; all that barking was a bit troubling. That's when I noticed a timid dog in the back that wasn't making a sound. That did it; *that* was the dog I wanted.

Jeff picked up the timid puppy and Pappaw put the dog in the car. After we got back to their house and I'd showed the puppy to Mammaw, we went outside and watched the pup wander around in the yard, making his way down to the persimmon tree by the road.

Pappaw and I followed, walking on down and then sitting on the retaining wall as we watched the dog underneath playing at our feet. I recall the wall was just below the hundred-year flood plain, and the bottom step of the porch was just above it. The river, being less than half a mile away, never made it up on the porch, and seldom came over the retaining wall.

As we watched, Pappaw asked me what I wanted to name the puppy. I don't think I had ever gotten to name the other dogs, and it was hard to think of anything. I asked Pappaw what was the name of the man we got the dog from; he said Jeff Buckner. I decided to name the dog after that man. And that's how Jeff the dog got his name.

Jeff went home with me that day when my parents came and got me. This was good, as I was already desperately attached to him. A few months later, in November of 1962, he moved with us when we moved to the Alvis place. He was with my Dad when he died in Feb '67, and he was with Mom and Darla and me when we moved to town in December of that same year.

Jeff only ever barked about three times in his whole life. He could hear and see and smell, and was capable of barking, but for some reason we never fathomed, he just didn't make much noise. Who knows, maybe he felt he didn't have to. He was a great dog, but a terrible coward, and so never made much of a cow dog or watch dog.

In 1964, we got another puppy named Blackie, who was some kind of terrier. He was bigger than a rat terrier, but still a small dog. Blackie never knew he was small, and he became a great watch dog. Every time Henry (our neighbor, and one of my Dad's best friends) came over, the dog would bite the cuff of Henry's pant leg and hang on as he kept walking to the door.

On the other hand, Jeff was jealous, but true to his personality he didn't initiate a direct conflict. He would lead Blackie far away from the house and then would run home, leaving Blackie to try to find his way home by himself. Several times my parents had to go find him. The poor pup would be exhausted and lost and several hundred yards away from the house after hours of searching for his way back.

Once he was gone for three days. We all thought that Jeff had finally defeated us, and then that night we heard a whine coming from the barn. My dad grabbed a flashlight and returned from the barn a few minutes later with an injured Blackie. The pads on his feet were worn, but he was limping from other injuries. Recently there had been a rash of state boy escape attempts (the State School, the juvenile detention center run by Texas, wasn't too far from us; you could see the lights for quite a distance), and my dad figured that a state boy had kicked him. That was the last time Jeff tried to lead Blackie off.

One day, Mom and Dad asked me if it would be okay for Jeff to go on a vacation to Pappaw and Mammaw's. In reality, they wanted to separate the dogs until Blackie could grow up and learn how to get home by himself. So that's why Jeff went back to Ater to stay for a while. We used to see him on Sundays when we came over to visit.

He was really pampered there. Mammaw even used to scramble eggs and make gravy and biscuits for him! Yes, she would fix Jeff breakfast. I guess between her and Pappaw there weren't that much table scraps unless she intentionally cooked a little extra. Talk about a "dog's life." Ol' Jeff had it made in the shade there.

Blackie was a resourceful dog. He used to open the screen door and come inside and get in my bed. Even with juvenile delinquents escaping from the minimum-security correction facility and terrorizing the countryside, in those days no one locked their doors. Mom would be laying in bed and hear the screen door open, and then hear the sounds of Blackie's little claws tapping on the linoleum in the hallway. She would then scold him to get out of the house.

One extremely hot day (this was the summer of '64, and the store in Arnett had a thermometer that read 110 degrees that day), my dad was plowing in the field. Blackie followed him around and around out there. When Daddy came home for dinner (lunch), he decided to sit on the couch on the screened in back porch for a while, digesting his food and resting.

Blackie took his nose and opened the screen. Coming inside, he softly laid his head down on Daddy's boots. Daddy and Mom realized right away something was wrong. And they were right. It was heat stroke. Blackie's front feet started to fail him, and he kept falling forward and convulsing and coughing.

Daddy rushed him back outside and used the water hose to try to cool him off; he even wet down Blackie's bedding in the dog house. In spite of their best efforts to cool the dog down, it was too late. In just minutes the heat stroke had killed Blackie.

Seeing this, my sister Darla started to cry, "I want my Backie back! I want my Backie back!" (she could not pronounce "Blackie"; she called him "Backie"). Blackie did not come back, but a few weeks later Jeff came back from vacation.

And we sure were glad to see him.

Speaking of heat, I have a lot of early summertime memories, and a lot of them revolve around our legendary Texas scorchers. They were simpler times, times with no air conditioning. And we really didn't miss what we didn't have.

People used to sweat. And I don't mean when working outside or exercising. I mean when just sitting still, or sleeping, or just about anything. Imagine having no air conditioner in your house or your car. Our summers were hot and our winters were cold. Houses then had lots of windows and high ceilings to keep things less hot in the summer, but that also made things less warm in the winter.

But if that's all you knew, you weren't so miserable; it was considered normal. In fact, air conditioners seemed abnormal to me. They felt cold, and made my head hurt (at least the refrigerator coolers—the ones running on Freon—did).

The swamp coolers (more formally called an evaporative cooler) were nice, but they didn't really do much unless you were right in front of them. For those who don't know, a swamp cooler is basically a large, box-like fan walled in by water-wetted pads; kind of poor man's AC. As I said, they worked after a fashion, but you practically had to be right on top of them, and in the middle a real Texas scorcher they usually came up short.

When I was an early adolescent, and more concerned about appearances, I began to be more willing to accept air conditioning. On days when everyone else seemed as fresh as a daisy, I was the only one damp from perspiration. That's when I grudgingly started to accept as a good thing the frigid air a good air conditioner can put out.

But in truth I believe it's made us a less hearty bunch, and now we find ourselves addicted to its artificial climate. Yearly we spend a small fortune on electricity to create those climates. And while we keep our windows shut and our curtains closed so we'll consume less electricity, we waste endless kilowatt hours burning lights in the day in our dark indoors. And it takes its toll on us in other ways as well. It seems we fritter away our time watching television, and never get to know our neighbors, people who are also locked away in their own climate-controlled isolation chambers they call home.

But it wasn't always this way. My Mammaw used to take a bath in the middle of the day just to cool off. She washed the porch a lot, not because it was dirty, but to cool down the warm concrete. She and Pappaw then would sit outside on the east porch in the evening and do nothing, just talk and watch an occasional car go by.

I think we've lost the joy of just sitting in place and doing nothing, listening to whippoorwills, doves, mockingbirds, rain crows, crickets, or whatever chorale God's creation has on stage that evening. Just sitting and rocking and talking and listening seemed boring to me as a youngster, but now it's a lost art that I want to re-discover.

From November 1962 to December 1967 my family leased about four hundred acres land called the Alvis Place. At the same time, my Dad leased another two hundred acres, also owned by Mrs. Alvis, so before it was done he toiled away on nearly six hundred acres.

My mom's parents lived on another spread called the Farris Place. There were a lot of big farm and ranch operations in Texas, and as a child my mom had lived most of her childhood on a large ranch (spreading out over sixteen hundred acres). Most likely her family had leased farmland from the ranch owners, and leased the attached house. The ranch hands used to look for cattle by airplane; it was that big. Once spotted, they would land, and then drive or ride horses to that part of the ranch to check on the cattle. The ranch was too large to just randomly go out looking for the critters. She used to joke that any boyfriend that came to date her had to be serious, because it took thirty minutes to drive to their house from the front gate, and if his car didn't have a squeak in it before, it would after he came down the road to her house.

Growing up in Coryell County, for some reason the Noah flood story sticks in my mind. Where we lived was on a prairie, not anywhere near an ocean, and not what one would call lowlands, yet we had petrified sea shells in our driveway.

The limestone outcrops on the side of the hill behind and above my Pappaw's house looked similar to a river bank, and his house was above any known flood zone of the river that bordered his place. The line of hills above his hill and miles farther away also looked like river banks to me. It was easy for me to believe that the world had been covered by water, in spite of the fact that water was a scarce and precious commodity at the time. Speaking of big places, the U.S. Army had Fort Hood, a base that consumed a large fraction of Coryell County Texas. It was heralded as the largest military installation in the free world. Which begged the question, did the non-free world have one bigger? I doubted it. Fort Hood is well over 50,000 acres!

While I'm thinking about it, we used to watch Army paratroopers practicing from our porch on the Voss place (and on the Alvis place). Actually my Mom and Dad would say "look", but all I ever saw were black dots. They told me they were people jumping out of airplanes; that's how close Fort Hood was.

My mom's ritual of dusting the shelves and putting the "what-nots" back in place had to be performed every week. If she went longer than that, the "what-nots" would walk off the shelf and crash on the floor. This was because of the vibrations of the big guns at Fort Hood. To us it sounded like thunder, and it was just part of the natural order of things in Coryell County.

At night, the soldiers practiced war games and would shoot big flares to light up the battlefield. We used to watch the magnesium light show in the southeastern sky, and listen to the thunder. Before they passed the law, we heard a lot of sonic booms in the day, but I don't remember them in the night. I guess months later while those Fort Hood guys were trying to sleep in the jungles in Vietnam, I was sleeping in my bedroom on the prairie to the same noises (but in different time zones of course).

My dad tried farming most of the Alvis Place, but now it looks more natural as pasture. I've heard it said that a Las Vegas gambler has nothing on a dry-land farmer. If you want to see a real dice-roller, take a look at one of them. For a dry-land farmer, gambling is a way of life. He gambles on when the soil is moist enough and not too dry and when it will rain again. He gambles against hail and drought and insects and skimpy harvests.

And still he calls himself a lucky man.

There was a seep near us (a shallow place where water collects) and some large cottonwood trees. Somewhere I have a picture of the place where we farmed, and in foreground is the land with the seep referred to as the lost ninety, a term which I mentioned earlier. The tract came by its name logically enough: it was a ninety-acre field that was very difficult to get to. You had to navigate the seep to get there, unless you came all the way around by the road. There is now a pond where the seep once was and in the background the old barn still stands near the place where the old house and chicken coops once stood. A new house stands there now.

The main road, Hwy 84, is about another half mile beyond the dwelling. To the left of the house and much further back is a blue ridgeline. It is a bench we called Pete Tharp Mountain. Another landmark near us was Hard Bargain Mountain although it would not have been visible from the lost ninety. I've learned over the years if you see a far ridgeline like that, it usually points in the direction of water. I know for a fact that's true, because the Leon River is between this location and that ridgeline. If you were on that bench you could get Dallas—Ft. Worth TV stations. With a view like that, you can understand my lack of appreciation for western Oregon.

As I said, by then Dad was farming and ranching close to six hundred acres, and doing so he caught a lot of people's attention. I have some funny recollections of him from that time.

Once he was supposed to be on the cover of *Progressive Farmer Magazine*, but refused to get his picture taken; why, I have no idea. Camera shy I guess.

Another time a student from India was going to come to the USA and live with us. He was going to learn about farming from my Dad, but he got lost and never showed up; we never did discover what became of him.

And yet another time we were watching the TV program *What's My Line?* It was a pretty famous game show of its era, and the premise was simple: celebrity contestants tried to guess the occupation of the guest. That night it turned out my dad and mom knew the guest; he sold ladybugs to farmers to eat aphids, and we'd bought some from him. We took the ladybugs and poured them into the planter, then broadcast them across the fields. Crazy, huh?

I've been saying how television strongly influenced my life, and it's true. Especially with what happened one fine spring day in 1962.

My mom was glued to the set. On it some men kept talking about a fellow that was going to ride on a rocket and fly around the world really fast. The man had a name; they talked about him a lot, and they used his name a lot: John Glenn. They said now that John had taken off he was going to fly real high, above the blue sky. They kept talking about where he was now, and where he was going to be next.

At that, Momma had a fit. She jumped up and ran outside, and said he was going to fly *right over our house*. She hollered for me come look. I came running outside, but neither of us saw anything but sky, and lots of it. I felt rooked. She soothed me by saying Mr. Glenn was up too high, and that was why we couldn't see him.

I was puzzled, but then many things about television—our lifeline to the world— puzzled me. For instance, I remember watching the *Beverly Hillbillies* show when I was very young. Not too strange, you might say, but this is: I thought when they waved at the end of each episode, that they were waving at me.

I recall one-time walking and looking behind the television to see where they went when the show was over. My parents tried to explain, saying that they weren't really inside the television in the first place. They said the Clampetts were just picture of people that were somewhere else. They said real people did not live inside the TV. So somehow Jed Clampett wasn't real, but John Glenn was. To me, that made no sense. I tried to understand how to discern what was real from what was not real. to figure it out. I guess it had a lot do with the adults in the room, and how they reacted to the television, but sometimes it had to do with whatever those grim men (news anchors) on the screen were talking about. When they talked, it was about something *real*. If they weren't on the screen, then the people there were just pretending. It was still puzzling to me.

I wondered how those men were able to tell the difference. I figured it had to do with those things they held up to their ears that they listened to, kind of like telephones. On the other end, I figured there had to be some obviously smart people telling them about what was real, and what wasn't. Sometimes they'd show the smart person, and he would talk to us; during the space race, they talked about Cape Canaveral a *lot*.

Much later in my life, my Grandded decided that the smart people must have been pretending too. He said that they were lying and that we didn't go to the moon. To me, this was amazing. How could they have fooled a whole country? Easy, he said; they took the cameras to Arizona and made up the whole thing.

My Grandded said a lot of funny things. He remarked that every time he saw the Pope on TV, it made his backside hurt. But there was one person on TV that Grandded thought never lied. He was smart enough to know when everybody else was telling a fib, and he would tell you what was really going on. That one person was Walter Cronkite. Grandded thought Uncle Walt had hung the moon. Who knows, maybe he did.

So let's look at the scorecard again.

Number one: John Glenn was real, even though we almost never saw him on TV, and we couldn't see him at *all* when he flew over our house.

Number two: Jed Clampett was *not* real, although we saw him every week (but he had a real pretty daughter and a nice dog, so maybe that made up for it).

Number three: although he was the leader of the Catholic Church, the Pope was bad.

And number four, Walter Cronkite was very good, because he was a straight-shooter. That was from Grandded's lips, and so it was Holy Writ.

Truth be told, I preferred Huntley-Brinkley over Uncle Walter, but since they also couldn't discern better than to trust the Pope, I could never understand how Walter could.

The most influence on me as a boy of five came from two TV programs. The first was *The Rifleman*, which I've already mentioned. It starred Chuck Connors as rancher Lucas McCain; Johnny Crawford played his boy, Mark. I thought they had the greatest life a father and son could have, always farming and ranching and hunting and fishing. Plus, Lucas got to plug the occasional crook with that fancy rifle of his, the one with the large round lever.

I'd always had a toy gun in my hand, and played cowboys and Indians and all kinds of shoot'em up games, including blasting away at bad guys on TV. But one day I made the mistake of having my gun pointed at the TV when Lucas McCain and his rifle made that hard stare at audience at the beginning of the program.

I was cooked. I knew he was looking right at me, and didn't appreciate the fact I had my six-shooter pointed at his craggy face. That was it. I backed down immediately. No way I was gonna go up against the Rifleman. I didn't care if he wasn't real. You just didn't want to take the chance.

But the other program came on years later in 1965, and it was another Chuck Connors show called *Branded*. It also influenced me greatly. As a young Texas boy, I knew how horrible it was to be labeled a coward; it meant you were a scaredy-cat or a sissy. And Jason McCord was certainly no coward, but was wrongly accused of being one. I felt bad for him. Chuck had already stared me down as the Rifleman and now here he was, considered a coward. It seemed a tough break. A what did it make me? Could it be that I had actually backed down from a coward? I still remember feeling very uncomfortable about the whole thing.

CHAPTER FOUR

◆

1963

I told you about the little church in the country where we worshipped until 1967 or 68, when we started going to church in town. I have not told you much about the preaching that went on in those little country churches. One reason is because I didn't listen very well.

Most of the time one of the men from the congregation would get up to preach. Many times, an older gentleman named Francis Saunders would do the honors. I don't remember anything he said, but he was generally liked by the folks that went there. Every summer we would have a revival, and some outsider would preach every evening for eight days straight (it started on Sunday and ended on the next Sunday). I liked revivals a lot, because the sermons would be livelier. I think the phrase that best describes the preaching used during those meetings is, "hellfire and brimstone." Sometimes you could really feel it too. I remember the guest preacher would ask a lot of rhetorical questions, the biggest being, "Are you ready for the Judgment Day?"

I sure hoped so. I hoped I was straight with both God and my folks, because I'd also had heard from my parents that God wanted me to obey them. About the only thing I really remembered at the time was them telling me to pick up my toys.

So, the best way I could figure of being ready for judgment was by having most of my toys already in the toy box. The rest of them I kept close enough so they could be easily tossed in as we dragged the box outside to board the glory cloud, headed for eternal bliss.

But I knew if a person was not prepared, he would face a terrible fate. I didn't know exactly what that terrible fate would be, but I imagined that it would be similar to those days when my mom would kill one hundred fryers and put them in the freezer.

Although I have never seen a chicken cry (and contrary to what you may have heard, chickens do not have teeth), the biblical phrase of "weeping and gnashing of teeth" and most other references to Judgment Day cause me to think about those times.

The quote "runnin' around like a chicken with your head cut off" means little unless you have seen a hundred barn fowl in your back yard, meeting their end at the hands of your mom. I always thought that those headless chickens had it in for me 'cause they always seemed to make a line for me on a dead run.

And that's funny phrase: "dead run;" I wonder if it originated from somebody watching a gory chicken kill. The chickens that still had their heads were not very calm while watching their recently departed brethren run by; Judgment Day must surely be a similar ordeal.

By the way, when it came time to pack 'em up, my dad didn't do a very good job putting the chicken parts in the freezer. Some packages would have three legs; some would have only one. It made for interesting suppers.

To carry this "Judgment Day" analogy a little further, my mom sold eggs to the grocery store, so I guess the chickens that didn't end up in the freezer and got to stay in the hen house were the ones judged to be righteous.

I always thought it was cool (cool being a hippie term that I didn't know yet, but adopted quickly from my cousin Randy that lived in Dallas; Dallas folks were more in the know) how we could go to the store and get groceries and the store would give us money.

Speaking of grocery stores and towns and all things non-rural, I still remember where I was the first time somebody asked me if I had ever heard of the Beatles. I was standing out in my cousin's pasture underneath an elm tree near a waterfall, and I laughed. I told my cousin that beetles didn't make any noise that I knew of. They told me it was a band. Puzzled, I asked why a band would name themselves after a bug.

Another cousin said it was a rock band and a lot of rock bands used drugs; maybe that was the reason. I had to ask what drugs were. They said it was like medicine. I then inquired what kind of sickness were they suffering from. They told me they weren't sick, they just took it anyway. So, I then asked why would anyone take medicine if they weren't sick?

The three of us didn't really know. I laughed to myself at something as absurd as people taking medicine when they weren't sick, and then naming themselves after bugs.

I absolutely had no desire to even investigate what this band sounded like. Months or years later (I have no way of knowing for sure) local teens started calling our radio station and denouncing the Beatles because they said they were more popular than Jesus. Absurd once again, because to my knowledge that station had never once played their music (or any rock song for that matter). At that time, I'd still never heard their music. I didn't feel I was missing much: people who took medicine when they weren't sick and had named themselves after a bug, and were now saying that they were greater than Jesus; that was one of the craziest things I'd ever heard.

Nationwide, by 1963 things were also changing as regards to race (I'll talk more about this later in the book) and gender. The Presidential Commission of the Status of Women presented disturbing facts about women's places in our society. In response, such women as Betty Friedan, Pauli Murray, and Gloria Steinem (who started the National Organization for Women) began questioning the unequal treatment of women.

This unease gave birth to the Women's Liberation Movement (often shorted to Women's Lib), and one of the things they discussed in excruciating detail was the "glass ceiling," or what was perceived to be a limit as to how far a woman could rise in a corporation. In our little Texas town, of course, they might as well have been speaking Martian. We knew what a woman's place was; *everybody* knew it … then.

There was also a thing we started hearing about on TV called the National Association for the Advancement of Colored People (which seemed like quite a mouthful; no wonder folks just usually called it by its acronym, the NAACP). This really came to the forefront was the year Dr. Martin Luther King Jr. made his famous "I have a dream" speech on August 28 of that year.

More than two hundred thousand peaceful demonstrators came to Washington DC to demand equal rights for blacks and whites. Part of the speech stated "I have a dream that my four little children will one day live in a nation where they will not be judged by the color of their skin but by the content of their character …"

If he could see us today, I wonder what he'd think.

Much of the political movements and the people participating in them came from the civil rights struggle in the south in the late 1950s and early 1960s. Blacks began to challenge segregation in the south through various means, such as boycotts, freedom rides, sit-ins, lawsuits, and registering blacks to vote.

From what I could gather from my parents and others, the goals were worthy, but the means to reach those goals sometimes was less than that. And there were people who didn't want them to succeed at all. As a case in point, Medgar Evers, an NAACP field secretary, was assassinated by a Ku Klux Klan member on June 12, 1963.

It was when I was five years old that I first began noticing that we Texans have our own way of saying things. The word for that is "slang", but I didn't find this out until years later. My mom's dad taught me a real good one, which I didn't use as a little boy in the Sixties, but have as an adult: WOW sorry, editor says I can't tell you. Sorry, my bad. My more colorful language evolved in the seventies and later.

Some of the Texas slang terms we used were darned near poetic: "bob wire" (barbed-wire); "cold enough to freeze the horns off a billy goat" (self-explanatory); "all" (meaning oil, the lubricant used in cars); "plowers" (a tool spelled P.L.I.E.R.S.); dinner, our term used in place of lunch; supper, our term used in place of dinner (confused yet?); plus different phrases for a large rain event, which we sometimes got a lot of in Texas: "rainin' cats and dogs", "gully washer", and "frog strangler" (my personal favorite).

Put them all together and you'd have something like, "Yesterday afternoon at dinner we got us a real frog-strangler; like to have washed the plowers clean out of my hand. Then an hour later it started blowin' somethin' fierce. The temperature dropped so quick it got cold enough to freeze the horns off a billy goat; the bob wire fence must be down in Amarillo." No wonder non-Texans have such a hard time getting what we say; we must sound like we're from a whole 'nother planet.

Speaking of another planet, that leads me to goat rodeos; I might as well tell you about them while I'm at it. Goat rodeos? Yep, that's what I said. They were fun, but really dirty. Man, I used to get chewed out for trying to ride goats in my church clothes.

I could never wait to change them when we rode up to my Uncle Troy's and Aunt Pearl's for Sunday dinner (lunch by today's terms). Most of the time Sunday lunch was at Mammaw's & Pappaw's, but sometimes we would go to Uncle Troy's.

He had a son, my cousin, named Troy Lee, or as I called him "Trawlee", and he was thirteen months older than me. As soon as we'd get there I would run in the front door of their house but instead of changing, I'd run right out the back door and Troy and I would head straight for the barn.

That's where the goats were, you see.

All our games were centered around being a cowboy, and goats filled the bill. While falling off a horse sounded painful, falling of a goat or sheep didn't sound so bad; you didn't fall as far, so it couldn't hurt much. The sheep didn't have handle bars (horns), so it was easier to catch a goat.

Once caught, though, staying on one was next to impossible; I quickly found out goats have tremendous acceleration. Still, though, we always had a blast. Until one fine Sunday, when disaster struck.

We were going along, whooping it up, when the goat I was riding bucked me off. That wasn't so bad; I had always managed to land in dry "stuff" (it was a barnyard, so you know the "stuff" I'm talking about). Once back on my feet, a quick dust-off and I was good to go.

But not this time.

I'd thought I was in the clear when I landed, only what I didn't realize was that I'd lost one of my cufflinks … in the "stuff". And there it remains to this day. I looked and looked, but it had vanished. To this day, somewhere in my Uncle's corrals, buried under really old "stuff", it's still there. I recall my mother being furious with me; I think that may have been the last rodeo in church clothes.

Rodeos were part of Texas country life, and so were tractors. My dad owned two old ones that he called "popping johnnies." The joke was he needed to hook up one to the other when the first one wouldn't start. He did not buy them new, so he most likely had a much older year model. In probably 1965 or so, Daddy bought a Ford 6000, which he loved. Then we had three tractors, and it was like we were rich. When he got it, he plowed almost non-stop for three days straight.

Summers there were blazing hot. I remember some days coming home from school, and the field along the road would be like sifted flour. My dad didn't know the meaning of quit. Many days he would be in the field before I got up in the morning, and when I went to bed at night I could still hear his tractor in the field in the distance.

On one of the John Deere tractors he mounted a radio, and he would turn it up real loud so he could hear it over the sound of the engine. Sometimes at night I could hear the rumble of the tractor and the sounds of the radio combined. But that wasn't so strange. Many people I knew listened to the World Series every year while sitting in a cotton patch.

Some of the soil in our parts was rocky. As the tractor rode over them, you could hear the stones clanking against the plows. And sometimes they could fool you. A big rock would appear as a small one. It might look like it was no larger than your fist, although it could be the tip of a rock as big as a house. That could tear up a plow blade in no time flat, and then precious hours would be lost making repairs to it. I often heard my parents and grandparents saying they wished they lived in the heart of the black land, where there were no rocks.

I did not know the word "rape" back then, so I couldn't fully express myself, but I sometimes thought my dad was raping the soil. I felt like rocks were supposed to stay in the ground, instead of being plowed up by farmers.

Of course, once they were plowed up they were fair game for a boy to throw at whatever target he chose. The first verse of Luke 19:39-40 (Today's New International Version), says, *Some of the Pharisees in the crowd said to Jesus, "Teacher, rebuke your disciples!"* That's followed by, *"I tell* you," he replied, "if they keep quiet, the stones will cry out." Or else end up in some boy's slingshot. That's what I thought, anyway. I mean, after all the rocks were already on the top of the ground, and I was merely moving them to another spot on the top of the ground. My parents reassured me that those rocks were moving towards the top of the ground anyway; Daddy was just helping get them there a little quicker.

———————————•———————————

Now I was five, and it was the eve of my sixth birthday. My mom had asked me what kind of cake and icing I wanted for my birthday. I had told her, but then I changed my order; I really couldn't decide.

She was in the kitchen working quickly for the upcoming party. As I was leaning up against the kitchen counter near the sink, changing my cake order for what had to have been the thirteenth time, my mother yelled at me to hush.

Then she ran across the kitchen and turned up the volume on the radio that was on top of the refrigerator (we didn't call it a refrigerator, we called it an ice box; but it wasn't really an ice box; that was a name left over from an earlier version of appliances). The radio was always on in my mom's kitchen any time she planned to stay in there for any length of time.

Shortly after turning the radio up, she listened only for a minute. I listened too, but I couldn't understand what was being said. The words made no sense. We found out later that on this day, November 22, 1963, President John F. Kennedy had been assassinated in Dallas while riding in a motorcade. His companion in the car, the governor of Texas, had been shot and wounded as well. What many believe to be the President's assassin, Lee Harvey Oswald, was never sent to trial; while being moved by police to a different jail, a strip bar owner named Jack Ruby shot Oswald. To this day, nobody knows for sure who killed President Kennedy.

My mom turned to me and said, "Go to the tractor shed and tell your father that the president has been shot."

As I said, to my small ears her words didn't mean anything. But I knew she was very serious and I knew I must obey because it was important. Dutifully I walked out of the kitchen out the back porch and down to the tractor shed.

When I reached the tractor shed, I found my father and our good neighbor Archie Necessary deep in a rapid-fire conversation. My father was on top of a tractor with a fuel nozzle inside the fuel tank, and Archie was standing on the ground looking up at him. As I said, they were quickly talking back and forth—men stuff, I guessed.

I waited for a break so I could fulfill my assignment given to me by my mother. Again, I had no comprehension about what Daddy and Archie were talking about. Growing impatient, I blurted out in a loud but monotone voice, "Daddy, Mommy told me to tell you that the President has been shot."

Instantly both men stopped talking, and their bodies froze. I was amazed at the power I had over them by saying this one simple sentence. The silence lasted for several moments.

Archie finally broke it when he said to my father in a laconic tone, "Well, I guess this means the Russians are coming." My father silently nodded in agreement.

I turned and walked to the house wondering what is a Russian; maybe they'd bring me something for my birthday. I'd always enjoyed having company over, but just from their body language Archie and Daddy wouldn't have been pleased about that idea.

I walked back in the house and asked my mom, "What is a Russian?"

She told me that they were a people in another country that did not like Americans and that we were Americans.

I wasn't happy that they did not like us and wondered why they did not like us. She tried to tell me that they were bad guys similar to the way the Germans used to be. Them, I'd heard of. Somewhere in my early life I'd seen some war movies (WWI or WWII movies; I really can't recall). Anyway, the Germans were the bad guys, and the Americans were the good guys, and that's all there was to it.

In my mind it was just like Westerns, good guys versus bad guys (and I should know, I used to play Cowboys and Indians a *lot*; yes, the Indians were the bad guys). Even though I'd heard there was some Indian in my family, I'd never felt conflicted about that; I thought maybe I might have some special Indian powers to walk quietly, or be able to sneak up on something or someone.

When I learned that my last name was of German descent, that *did* make me feel conflicted. I knew the score: the Germans lost both wars, and were the bad guys. At least with Indians there were some good ones like the one that helped the Lone Ranger; I didn't know of any good Germans that weren't already in America.

But back to the event that day. I asked Momma, "What's a president?"

She told me he was a leader of the American people. Before I could ask anymore questions my father walked in and my Mom and him started talking.

I didn't understand what was going on, and they wouldn't tell me when the Russians would arrive. But it didn't matter: since now I knew they didn't like us, I was pretty sure they wouldn't be coming to my birthday party anyway. And even if they did come, they certainly would only want cake, and wouldn't bring me a present.

My mom says we had my party the next day, but to me it seems like it was in a different year. Weirdly enough, I remember it as the best party I ever had.

Lots of children came, and I got some plastic helicopters with some Mercury capsules just like the ones that the astronauts flew in and then splashed into the ocean. In fact,

Marlene and Garlene's mom accidentally got me a duplicate set of helicopters and capsules. They told my Mom we could take it back to the store if I wanted, but I refused. It was absolutely the greatest toy, and the more helicopters and capsules, the better.

The cake was really, really good too. My baby sister Darla also got a cake and some presents (her birthday—her second—was right after mine, on November thirtieth, so my mom had combined the parties). Darla's cake was in the shape of a lamb; she had a toy lamb that was her favorite toy.

Somehow as clear as all these memories are, the following events seem even clearer, probably because they were also on TV. They don't even seem tied to the same day, or week or year, although they were.

The day after my birthday we went to visit my Uncle Troy and Aunt Pearl. We drove up to the house and knocked on the front door, but nobody came to see who was there.

Finally they opened the door, and after apologizing for not answering our knock sooner, they quickly ran back to the television. As we were coming inside they explained that the man who shot the president had himself been shot right on television, just as we were knocking on the door. Amazed, we all stood in front of the set.

The people on the TV were very excited, and I knew something serious was happening. I could tell by the way the announcer was talking and by the way the adults in the room were acting as well.

A couple of days later Saturday came and I got up to watch cartoons, but to my anger and dismay they weren't on. Instead they were having the president's funeral. It wasn't as good as cartoons at first, but then I learned that the president had a little girl the same age as me and a little boy the same age as my sister Darla.

I didn't know the meanings of the words *pomp* or *ceremony*, but the importance of what was going on began to sink into my six-year-old mind. Something very important had happened and all the adults were sad because somebody very important had died. All people everywhere were united in agreement that something big had occurred.

The President's kids Caroline and John-John seemed very brave about it all, and I recall their mom wearing a black veil. Mommy said it was because she was mourning and she was sad and probably crying and that was what people do when they are mourning.

Caroline and John-John didn't have veils, and I didn't see them cry. Although I knew somehow Caroline was aware of what was going on and was sad too, John-John was like my sister: he was too little to understand. I remember a horse with no rider, and a saddle on its back with black shiny boots facing backwards in the stirrups. There was a horse-drawn carriage with the President's casket, and John-John saluted as it went by.

Three years and three months later I would be at my own father's funeral, and my connection to Caroline and John-John would be eternal.

CHAPTER FIVE

◆

1964

This year saw the arrival to our shores of the Beatles, a British rock and roll band that spearheaded the first "British Invasion". They became very popular, especially when they were seen on the Ed Sullivan Show. The music of the "Fab Four," as they were called—John Lennon, Paul McCartney, George Harrison, and Ringo Starr—was played on radio stations all over the world. They performed concerts that were quickly sold out. All the frenzy over the group became known as "Beatlemania", which was only the beginning of craziness that would last for years.

And I guess we needed crazy music to handle the stresses of the changes the country was undergoing. For instance, by late 1964 the first civil rights bill had been passed to stop racial discrimination in the United States; it was later amended to include gender. The civil rights movement made great changes in society in the 1960's … some good, some not so good.

The movement began peacefully enough, with Dr. Martin Luther King and Stokely Carmichael leading sit-ins and protests, where they were joined by whites and Jews. But while they were going about it peacefully, others weren't quite so forgiving. The controversial leader Malcolm X preached about Black Nationalism, which included statements that made an awful lot of white people very uncomfortable. After his assassination on February 21, 1965, the Black Panthers were formed to continue his mission; we all know how well that worked out.

Stimulated by this movement, but growing beyond it, were large numbers of student-age youth telling us what *they* wanted. It began with the Free Speech Movement at the University of California, Berkeley in 1964, and peaked four years later in the street riots at the 1968 Democratic National Convention in Chicago. To many historians the movement came to a climax with the shootings at Kent State University in 1970, which some claimed as proof that *"police brutality"* was rampant.

The terms the mouthy students used then included *"The Establishment,"* which referred to traditional management or government, and *"pigs,"* which was a slam against police using what they perceived to be excessive force. But some law enforcement personnel took that pejorative term and stood it on its head, stating that "pig" stood for pride, integrity, and guts. I kinda like that.

This was the year I entered first grade as a charter student of Gatesville Public schools, and Mrs. Hallmark was my teacher. I liked her okay, but I think she must have spanked the black boy in our class every day. She wasn't a racist; it's just that the kid, Billy Cameron (name changed to protect the innocent), had a real knack of getting on her bad side. I believe he may have failed the first grade the year before, and maybe she expected a lot more out of him this time around.

A lot of kids cried the first two weeks of school. I didn't until about the third week. When queried I said I didn't like standing in line; still don't. Not liking "standing in line" was the only way I knew to describe the conformity that I felt. It was so uncomfortable and oppressive. I never liked school, and I can really get on a soapbox about the public education system. Anyway, my mom complained to me that I was not playing or socializing there. She said she could tell, because when I came home my clothes were still clean. The next day I didn't play, but I did roll around on the ground on the playground like a horse taking a dirt bath. When I came home she was satisfied. But I eventually told her what I did.

In November of that year I had to go to school on my birthday. I thought that was extremely unfair; to my thinking, if your birthday fell on a school day, well, that was just too bad for the school. Oddly, my parents didn't see it that way, and made me go anyway.

I took one of my presents that day; I think it was some sort of James Bond toy. It looked like a transistor radio, but with a few surprises. Its size was big, almost 8" x 10" (but maybe not that big), and I remember you held it by the handle, which also turned out to be the scope of a weapon. With a flick of a switch on the top near the handle, a gun barrel came out from the side, and the bottom three-quarters of the body folded out to be a shoulder stock … kind of a switch blade gun, so to speak. Can you imagine a child in today's world trying to bring that in to a school? Neither can I. It may still be on some Mattel toy history website, but I've not found it.

By the way, I was not a GI Joe fan. To my thinking, boys didn't play with dolls. Sorry, just 'cause he's got on army fatigues, he's still a doll. I know a lot of my friends did the GI Joe thing—and admittedly using firecrackers with your GI Joe was a pretty cool adaptation—but it was just not my cup of tea.

In the end it really didn't matter what they did; before age seven I usually played alone. Why? Simple. Because I *was* alone. But that was okay. I had a lot of imaginary posse members that helped me ride out in search of the bad guys, kind of like Roy Rogers or the Lone Ranger or any of those shows. There was always a posse, but somehow the hero ended up facing the bad guys alone. Just like me.

And this brings me to another tale.

Perhaps you have seen one of those PBS nature documentaries, or better yet you may have witnessed a small animal that is suddenly captured by a hawk or an eagle, and is helplessly carried away in the blink of an eye. My mother-in–law saw that very thing for real, when one time she was sitting on her back patio in the cool of an Arizona desert morning. As she drank her coffee, she was watching a dove on the back fence.

Suddenly there was a harsh flutter, and then there was nothing left but some loose feathers floating to the ground. A hawk had dive-bombed and seized the unsuspecting bird and carried it away, never to be seen again.

In like fashion, so goes the tale of Chuck McLean. We were in the first grade and I was still trying to get my bearings on this thing called school. There were so many *rules*. In 1964 no one had heard of daycare, and kindergarten was optional. The first grade was rough. I guess it was my first exposure to the cold cruel world.

I was six years old, nearly seven, and didn't much care for it. Neither did anyone I knew. *Folsom Prison Blues* by Johnny Cash became a sort of anthem about the situation for us elementary school kids. I wasn't at all sure about this school thing, and had a lot of questions. I remember one exchange with my mother. It went something like this:

"Mom, why do I have to go to school?"

"To learn."

"Why can't you teach me?"

"Because teachers are better at it."

"Why?"

"Because I could only teach you what I know, and they are trained to teach you things I don't know."

"Are teachers smarter than you?"

"No."

"Then why do they know stuff that you don't know?"

"Well, I know it but I don't remember it all 'cause I don't use it every day. They learned things, and teach it to others every day so they remember it better and can teach it to you."

"Who taught it to the teachers?"

"Other teachers."

"Who taught the teachers that taught the teachers?"

"More teachers."

"Who taught the teachers that taught the teachers that taught the teachers?"

"Older teachers that learned it from other teachers that lived a long time ago."

"Who taught those teachers?"

"There were always earlier teachers that taught it to later teachers."

"Was Adam and Eve a teacher?

"No."

"I thought you said there were always teachers."

"Well, at first parents taught their children, but they could only teach them to be what they were. If they were a farmer, then their children were taught to be farmers. A child could only learn how to do what his parents had learned how to do. So, they made teachers to teach the children how to do other things."

"How do you know that the teachers that taught the teachers that taught all the teachers learned it right?"

"Well, if they did not learn it right or teach it right, then nobody would know how to do anything right."

"How do you know if they're doing it right? You said you don't use it everyday and you don't remember as much as the teachers. So how do you know if they're teaching it right?"

No response from Mom. Judging from what I see coming out of public schools and colleges these days, maybe we should go back to apprenticeship.

I still didn't seem to get the big deal about school. There was so much to it, just about more than a boy could stand.

There were school buses and standing in line to go the cafeteria and no time to eat and lines to go back to the room and nap times and this thing called recess. There were times for everything and standing in line for everything and letters to learn and songs to sing and words to read. There were lots of rules and lots of structure and lots of children.

As a boy who had always lived only with Mom and Dad and a little sister, and only saw others at the Auction Barn on Saturday, or church on Sunday, or at the grocery store on Tuesday where we sold eggs, it was a lot to take in and adjust to.

Each class had about thirty children, and there were five classes in each grade. At recess, we were allowed to go outside and play, so I guess there were at least a hundred and fifty kids on the playground at any one time.

Each group was supposed to stay in a certain area of the playground. My class was assigned an area near the road, or driveway; it was used by the school buses. There were no other cars on that road, but we all knew that we could not play in or near it.

One day while at recess a boy (I later learned his name was Chuck McLean) walked up to our group. I had never seen him before. Whoever he was, he seemed to be very comfortable and self-confident.

Right about then another boy discovered an empty glass jar on the playground. We were all very concerned about it, and wondered what we should do. Plainly, this was not supposed to be here. We all decided the best thing would be to give it to a teacher. She would know what to do, and we could tell her where we found it, all the time assuring her that we did not bring this forbidden item on to the playground.

But Chuck had other ideas. He confidently explained that since the jar was *not* school property, it had to be removed *from* school property. He then went on to explain that it would be impossible to get in trouble for breaking it, if it wasn't broken on school property. Well, maybe, but we reminded him that we were not allowed to leave the area.   But confident Chuck had an answer for everything. He pointed to the road, and in a reasonable tone said that it was not part of school. I called him on that. I stated that it was the school bus road, and since only school buses drove on it, it must be part of the school.

But Chuck had an answer for that too. He informed me that his mom drove on it everyday before and after school, and she didn't work for the school. He said since it was public property, that if he felt like it he could throw the glass jar right into the street and everything would be fine.

He laid it all out as evenly a philosophy professor. Chuck said he would get the pleasure of breaking the jar, the forbidden item would be removed from the school property, and we could all watch without ever leaving the area. Perfect, right?

He didn't give us a chance to answer. While we were mulling this over, he simply said "watch," and then gave the jar his most mighty heave. It landed about as hard as you would expect, crashing into a million pieces in the exact middle of the street. As our jaws dropped in astonishment, Chuck smugly said, "see?"

And see we did, as not one, but two teachers—who must have materialized from the earth behind us—grabbed him, one on each arm, and whisked him away as quickly and efficiently as any eagle or hawk would seize their unsuspecting prey.

I never saw Chuck McLean again until the third grade.

So school was a pain, but I still had church, and as I've said, I liked it. But sometimes, even there are things didn't always go quite right.

Once we had one of the visiting preachers over along with the whole congregation for an ice cream supper. I remember the ice cream not tasting quite right. That was when I found half of a candle bug in my bowl of ice cream.

Another time there I fell to sleep when I bowed my head to pray; hey, it happens. My head was resting on my folded arms that I'd placed on the back of the pew in front of me, and immediately I started dreaming that I was swinging on a swing.

I dreamed I was pumping the swing and getting higher and higher. I could see the ground and it was getting closer again. In an effort to reach maximum velocity and height I planned to push with my feet as I reached the point closest to the ground.

Just when I pushed what I thought was the ground, the large boom of my feet stomping the wooden floor woke me up. As I raised my startled head, the man leading the prayer said "Amen." Oddly enough, I never got in as much trouble there as I did for fidgeting. When I was younger I was escorted outside countless times for gritching around on the pew. Now with this performance all I received were stares from the whole congregation.

By the way, the ceiling fans in that church didn't seem to work very well. Many times in the summer months I remember not even feeling a breeze, and being as hot as blazes. I would look up from my pew at those blades turning and wonder why in the world I couldn't feel any air moving toward me. I deduced that I was just too short, and only the adults could feel the faint breeze provided (if there was any to be felt at all).

I believe I'd mentioned the folks at church used to say one day I would grow up to be either a preacher or a politician. I didn't become either one, but to this day I certainly don't mind talking about religion or politics.

In addition to church, I had my friends and family, and that brings me to the Twin Towers. But these aren't the ones you're familiar with. Theses days when one hears the phrase "twin towers", they usually think of the two tall buildings in New York City that fell to terrorists on September 11th 2001. On the other hand, if one is a pro basketball fan, and especially a San Antonio Spurs fan (I'm not; I like the Dallas Mavericks or the Boston Celtics), they may think of Tim Duncan and David Robinson.

But I want to talk about two other twin towers, Troy Don and Troy Lee (or TD and TL, as I'll call them). They were both only one year older than me; TD was the son of my parent's friends, and was a friend of mine, and TL was my cousin (my Uncle Troy and Aunt Pearl's boy). At age eight, and even younger, these were the big towers in my life.

Troy Don started driving a tractor by himself at age eight, and by then was doing all kinds of farm work at that young age as well. I was only seven, and I was afraid. I felt inferior because they were both doing "men's work", and I wasn't. This feeling of inferiority was compounded because not only were they doing something like that and I wasn't, but I was afraid to even try it. And the feelings only got worse when I was age nine, they had already done it for at least two years, and I still had yet to begin.

And it got worse. When my father died, I knew then I would never get the opportunity to drive the tractor. I was scared to, but at the same time wanted to, and I was envious of those that did.

The "twin towers" could run faster than me, jump higher than me, and drive tractors and grain trucks and play football, while my only remarkable trait was that I was smart. They got to do all kinds of dangerous stuff (and were brave), while I was afraid, and all I got was good grades.

The amount of anxiety and anger and envy caused by my comparison of myself to the twin towers and others like them seemed almost infinite. I really developed a self-esteem problem. It has affected me my entire life.

What did that make me? I lived in the shadow of the twin towers, and there was no getting away from that fact. Years later as I struggled to change an oil filter at age eighteen, or a light bulb at thirty, or any other small thing requiring manual dexterity I found myself comparing my efforts to the twin towers. And I felt so small and so insignificant. My accomplishments, though good, meant little to me; somehow, I would have rather been doing what they were.

Of course, in my mind, Troy Don (my friend) and Troy Lee (my cousin) could ride bikes and horses as easily as a bird in flight. Plus, as I said they could drive (yes, even at those young ages; it seems the rules were different for farm kids). At any rate, it made me feel very inadequate, even though the boys were in no way responsible. Troy Don and Troy Lee were beginning to do other things besides play baseball and football.

They were working, not just using a hoe to chop Johnson grass out of the cotton, like I did; not just riding in the back of a cotton trailer and using a pitchfork to toss the cotton further back in the trailer. No, they were driving tractors and trucks, real farm implements. My out (and I needed it) was that I was still too young to operate machinery. But even then, that rang false to my ears. So big deal that I got to use a hoe and a pitch fork; maybe I could save up my money and buy a stick horse to ride, just like the runt and almost useless kid I was. Yes, I know, not true. I've been to therapy.

CHAPTER SIX

◆

1965

Now it was 1965, and I was starting to understand a little about how fast science was changing things (not so much in Gatesville, you understand, but we still heard about it). A short time before, in 1961, physicist Theodore Maiman perfected the laser at the Hughes Laboratories, which of course is now widely used in surgery, holography, communications, and printing. And then in 1964 Douglas Englehart of Stanford University developed the computer mouse, along with a five key "corded" keyboard.

And then just three years later in 1967 the first hand-held calculator was invented by Texas Instruments (go Texas!), at a cost of $2,500 a piece … as you might imagine, nobody we knew owned one. That same year Dr. Denton Cooley implanted the first artificial heart in a human, and it kept the patient alive for three days until a human heart could be transplanted (which interestingly *also* happened that same year, when the first heart transplant was performed by Dr. Christiaan Barnard in Cape Town, South Africa).

1965 was the year that Sony began marketing the CV-2000, the first home video tape recorder. It was huge, clunky, and expensive, more of a novelty than anything else. We couldn't have known then that twenty years later nearly every home in America would have one, or that twenty years after *that* they'd be as obsolete as Model Ts.

This was also the year singer Bob Dylan went electric at the 1965 Newport Folk Festival. Later that summer he was called "Judas" for doing so by an irate audience member during the legendary Manchester Free Trade Hall concert.

The start of the bootleg recording industry followed, with recordings of this concert circulating for thirty years that had been wrongly labeled as *The Royal Albert Hall Concert*. It finally was legitimately released in 1998 as *The Bootleg Series Vol. 4: Bob Dylan Live 1966, The "Royal Albert Hall" Concert* … which was a mouthful.

Medicine and dentistry were also making big strides … too late to help my grandparent's teeth, unfortunately. Dentistry was different back in the Sixties. A great deal of old people had false teeth. There were no such thing as dental implants; at least if they existed, I didn't know or hear of anyone that had them.

That meant if people had false teeth they were the portable kind. Every time I went to my Grandded and Grandma's house and spent the night, I would see their teeth soaking in a glass of water. Grandded used to tease his grandchildren by pulling his teeth out of his mouth and then putting them back in, and then challenge us to pull our teeth out of our own mouths; we couldn't, which caused him much merriment.

Once we had tried unsuccessfully he would then give a second offer for us to reach in his mouth and pull his teeth out. I never dared.

You might not believe this, but my parents had a dentist to help pull my baby teeth when they got loose. I never knew of anyone getting their baby teeth pulled by a dentist but me. I think my dentist had the biggest thumb of any person on earth. I had heard all my life of dentists that had put fillings in people's teeth that didn't need them. To my thinking dentists rated down on the credibility scale along with lawyers and used car salesman. Most people I knew wouldn't go to a dentist unless it was an absolute necessity. Apparently the bigger their fingers and thumbs the more credible a dentist they were. Mom claimed our dentist was very credible. Could be. All I know was he had humongous fingers and thumbs and I gagged every time he stuck his hand in my mouth.

Grandded used to tell a story of an old man who had a problem with his false teeth fitting too loose. One cold day when there was ice covering the pavement around the courthouse, the old man was leaving the courthouse lawn when suddenly he sneezed. As he did his teeth flew out of his mouth and slid all the way across the street.

The man was so embarrassed; he made his way across the slick street, reached down, picked them up and stuck them back in his mouth without even taking the time to clean them off. They were probably dirty and may have been cold. I know first hand about some cold teeth. Not mine but my Mammaw's.

When Pappaw and Mammaw were still living on the river, Pappaw always tried to maximize how much acreage he could plant. This meant he often ended up having his tractor slide down the bank, where it would get stuck in the river.

Mammaw was constantly worrying about him. Once he had the tractor near the pump house in the yard and ran the machine up on the wood pile. I'm not sure what ignited; probably dry grass and heat from the tractor created a small fire underneath the tractor.

Anyway, Mammaw was in the kitchen preparing dinner when she heard Pappaw yelling and running to the house to get the water hose. She dropped what she was doing and joined my father and Pappaw to put the fire out. After the blaze was extinguished and the tractor was saved once again, they came back inside (I had been instructed to stay in the house for safety in case the tractor exploded; don't laugh, it could happen).

When Mammaw started to resume cooking, she realized that she didn't have her teeth in her mouth. She retraced her steps back to the wood pile and pump house and all over the kitchen and house, but she couldn't find her dentures anywhere. That's when she decided that she must have swallowed her teeth during all the trauma.

Reluctantly and sadly she began preparing dinner. Every now and then she would stop and inquire about what would happen to dentures in her stomach. Would she be OK? More importantly, would her teeth be OK? Finally, she finished cooking and went to the fridge to get ice for the tea glasses.

And there her teeth were, in the freezer portion of the refrigerator.

No one ever knew for sure how or why her teeth ended up in the freezer. We suspect she was putting ice cube trays in the freezer when she learned of the fire. Subconsciously she must have thought it was better to fight fire without her teeth.

And speaking of fighting fire, things were heating up for us, war-wise. President Johnson had started ordered bombing raids on North Vietnam, and Americans began protesting the war in earnest. Up until then it had largely been a secret war. That stopped when massive troop buildups were ordered to put an end to the conflict.

The draft was accelerated and anti-war sentiment began growing in the US. College students organized anti-war protests, draft dodgers started fleeing to Canada, and uneasy reports began surfacing of soldiers reflecting the growing disrespect for authority and shooting their officers rather than follow orders.

The civil rights problems were still going on here at home. This was the year the Watts riots broke out in Los Angeles. This was also when the term "blacks" became socially acceptable, replacing "Negroes."

In 1965, I was going into second grade. My teacher that year was Mrs. Casey. She was really sweet, and kind of grandma-like. I'd really wanted get Mrs. Poston, who was fresh out of college, but Mrs. Casey was great as a second choice.

Something weird about that year was that was the first time I realized I'd never learned to tie shoes. But it was no big deal; I'd never had the need to learn how. I didn't even own any tennis shoes (or as I called them "shoes with strings") until I signed up to play baseball. Up until that point I had either worn boots, or gone barefoot. You can't learn to tie shoes if you had never had any "with strings."

I was now eight years old, and I still wasn't driving, like the "twin towers" I told you that Troy Don and Troy Lee drove. Can you imagine how absurd I felt to be eight and still not driving? Plus, they had horses. Real horses, not imaginary ones.

But it was okay. I now had a horse to ride, and her name was Old Betty.

There are pictures of me on Old Betty dated sometime in 1966, but I think we may have had the horse a year earlier. Daddy had asked Lloyd Cathey to sell him a good kid horse. Lloyd said he wouldn't sell him one or give him one, but he would let him keep one until he got tired of it, and then he would want it back.

That was just the kind of man he was. Lloyd was a real cowboy, and Betty—the horse he gave us—was a real horse (emphasis on real, not just a pony that one might rent for a party). No, Betty was the real deal, and not a short horse either.

From her I learned that horses really do have "horse sense." A horse like Betty has their own personality, and their own ideas. A kid could climb on Betty's back, saddles or bareback it didn't matter, and she stayed steady. Either way it was like climbing on a statue.

It was really hard to get her to do anything. Betty pretty much knew if you were smart enough to make her work. A kid could try as hard as they could, and if he was lucky, she would walk. On the other hand, if an adult would climb in the saddle, they had better be ready for the ride of their life.

You see, Old Betty was a "cuttin' horse," which meant her job on the ranch was to cut out cows from the rest of the herd. When someone of any real size got on her back, she thought they wanted to go to work. She could turn, or as we say "cut", so sharply that when my father would ride her, his leg would drag the ground as the horse leaned into the turn. Later my dad would grab that leg, complaining of soreness and bruising from about the top of the boot on down. And you could tell he was hurting from above the ankle to below the shinbone on that side.

Betty was fast and agile, but as the "old" part of her name said, she was getting on in years. She was only good for one day, and then she would have to rest up for a few days before she would be able to work like that again. And that's why she had been relegated to the position of being a good "kid horse."

A kid horse is one that is smart enough not to hurt their rider, while being savvy enough to know how to get out of dangerous situations, or better yet, to avoid them. I've heard folks say about these types of horses, "If you get in a tight spot, just drop the reins and let the horse figure out what to do. Just hold on to the saddle horn, and she'll take you home." This is not unlike the story I told earlier, of the horse my grandmother rode when she was five.

Anyway, I found this old mare a bit frustrating. She wouldn't always do what I wanted. Plus, she knew how to open gates. I got in trouble several times when I was accused of leaving the gate open and letting the horse get out. My parents thought I was being insubordinate because I denied leaving the gate open.

But one day my father and my mother told me they were sorry; they'd seen for themselves I was telling the truth. That afternoon they were setting on the back porch when they saw Betty walk up to the gate and bite the chain and shake her head until she had shaken the chain off the nail. The horse stepped away and let the gate swing back. She then walked around the half-opened gate and proceeded on to the greener grass on the other side of the fence.

I loved, and still do love the idea of riding horses, especially bareback, although I'm way out of practice and out of shape for that kind of thing now. It is almost a religious experience to ride a horse bareback and barefooted, as if all the plains Indians are raised from the dead, and you're riding along with that ghost tribe. The feeling of the bottom of your feet pressing on the hairy horse hide causes your brain to tap into the horse and the prairie and the essence of the hopes and dreams of any other barefoot rider before you. It's not necessarily an exhilarating experience, but more a comforting and simultaneously liberating feeling.

Today I know a lady that uses horses as therapy for children with disabilities like autism. I can't explain the science behind it, but to see what I mean, just one time you should ride a horse bareback and barefooted. Then you, too, will know it works. A horse is a mysterious creature; perhaps a pre-adolescent boy with a big imagination is too.

I received a bicycle one Christmas, but I had a hard time learning to ride it on the bumpy rocky road at the farm. There were no nice sidewalks where I was at. Another thing about bicycles back then: boys' bikes had a bar running from the seat to the handlebars, and that was all too often an instrument of pain for our gender. Hit a rock, slide off the seat, and the pain would nail you "right where you lived." Girls' bikes didn't have that tortuous feature. Allegedly that bar wasn't on their bikes because it prevented their dresses from draping, as any proper female would not want their dress or skirt to catch the wind and go flying up.

Now these "features/variations" on the frame have lost their meaning, because no one wears a dress these days, especially females. The ERA movement had not happened back then. I had scornfully told my folks I was a cowboy, and needed a horse. I'd cursed that old bicycle. Now with Old Betty, I had a horse I couldn't control either.

But I have another animal story to tell you from that year, and this one is—excuse the term—a real "stinker." It happened when I was eight years old and playing in the garden with my shooter; that word requires a bit of explanation.

Now don't be shocked, but in 1965 the only word I knew for my shooter was "black shooter." Only the word was not "black". Many children back then held no animus towards another race, they simply knew no other word to use. I know that seems hard to believe but it is true. Some people called them slingshots, but technically it was *not* a sling shot. That was what David had shot Goliath with, and that was a device that one swung around in a circle before letting go of one part, releasing a rock. I never intended to shoot blacks with it, so I never really knew what to call one of my favorite toys. That word which is no longer uttered was just a word used mostly by older people, but a word momma said we couldn't say at school 'cause it might start a fight. What I had was a Y-shaped stick with a long elastic band.

I was out in the garden one day looking for some rocks that had been plowed up, and doing a little target practice on the pickets in the fence. That's when I spotted a skunk walking from the hog pen straight to the garden. I looked for a way of escape and realized that I was trapped.

I could not climb over the picket fence, and I feared the skunk would spray me as I exited the garden as he entered it through the only gate. Reaching down, I grabbed a stone and tried to shoot the critter with my shooter. As a summer activity, I'd thrown rocks at chimney swifts, and figured this couldn't be any harder than that. But no; I'd led him a little too much and missed his nose by inches. Once more I shot, and the rock flew over him.

That was it. I now ran as fast as I could for the gate, just barely beating the skunk to the entrance. I was in his range but there was a woodpile between the skunk and me. The animal really did not sense any danger and didn't attempt to spray me; thank God for small favors!

Out of breath I ran in the house and told my mom and dad about my life-threatening ordeal. They were both in the kitchen, and my mom appeared fairly unconcerned. She was just glad that I had missed the skunk. But my dad seemed very interested, and wanted more details about the animal and which direction it was headed.   But he took it a step further. My dad went outside and started looking for it. Some time later he came back and reported to Mom that he'd found a hole in the ground near one of the chicken houses. Bear in mind, skunks don't eat chickens, but for some reason, they *will* sometimes bite their heads off. I have no idea why, and that's why my dad was so concerned. Anyway, he told her that he thought the skunks had made a den near the chicken house where we kept the baby chickens.

In my little-boy thinking, I imagined that the skunks lived in a below-ground apartment, and would simply walk out of the hole when hungry for chicken, just as one would order a pizza by phone today. The next day my dad went to town and bought a trap, which he placed near the hole.

It didn't take long for activity to occur.

Each night the trap would catch a skunk, which in a blind panic would spray the side of the chicken house; each night my father would then walk out to the trap and shoot it. This occurred every night for two weeks (yes, daddy killed fourteen skunks from that hole).

But trouble occurred on night ten.

The trapped snapped shut and the skunk sprayed and daddy shot just as every other night. Except that on this night the skunk sprayed my father instead of the side of the chicken house.

My dad came to the house gagging and coughing, and mommy, appalled at the stench, made him strip all his clothes off outside. She then filled the bathtub full of water and poured a bottle of Aqua Velva men's cologne in the water. Dad walked through the house and took that bath, but it only made him smell like a skunk wearing Aqua Velva. That night mom made him sleep on the back porch. It was a screened in deal, and the dog usually slept just outside the screen door on the top step. We could never open that door until we had shooed the dog from it. On this night dad smelled so bad that the dog wouldn't even sleep with him. That night, our dog slept on the front porch.

Chapter Seven

1966

Popular music was evolving rapidly. The Beach Boys released *Pet Sounds* in 1966, ushering in the era of album-orientated rock. In February of the same year Frank's daughter Nancy Sinatra's song, "These Boots Are Made for Walkin'," became very popular. This was also the year *The Supremes A' Go-Go* became the first album by a female group to reach the top position of the *Billboard* magazine pop albums chart in the United States.

In geo-political terms, by 1966 things that had been in a relatively slow simmer worldwide were beginning to boil. With the draft securely in place, we now had more than five hundred thousand troops in Vietnam—boots on the ground (and in the air)—sent there by the Johnson administration.

In the summer of that year an event occurred to me that wouldn't bear complete fruit until the November of the following year. I was in the house, and headed for the back-screen door to go out and play. My mom was straightening up the place, and told me to pick something up. I had already moved way past her and was at the screen door, and it would have been very plausible that I did not hear her. I could have convinced her or any jury in the land that I did not hear her. But the fact was that I did hear her. I turned around and did exactly what she told me to do.

After the small task was done, I headed back to the screen door. Just as I raised my hand and pushed on the door, a thought passed through my mind: "I wish I could be bad like other kids and not mind (obey). No one would have known I'd really heard her, and I could have done the task later after I had gone back inside."

The thought had completed itself as I was outside on the steps. As I reached the bottom step and turned left toward the swings, it felt as though a hand was sternly placed on my shoulder and turned me around swiftly.

Spinning around, I looked up to see who had grabbed my attention. There was no one there, and my gaze was drawn to a blinding afternoon sun. I put my hand up to block it, looking around, but no one was there. Yet I experienced a presence and a conviction.

I felt guilty and alone, though I had done nothing wrong. I knew what I had just thought was something wrong. I tried reasoning within myself that I should not feel guilty for obedience, but the simple thought of *wishing* to be bad was convicting me. And not just a conviction, but now loneliness was enveloping me, in spite of the feeling that someone perhaps from heaven had just spun me around and had forced me to gaze straight into the sun. I was not struck blind and I did not hear a voice like the apostle Paul on the road to Damascus, but there was a similarity, although on a much smaller scale.

I turned around and went on to the swings. By the way, the swings had wood seats and were made of good chains and were secured to a heavy pipe frame. It was almost impossible to swing high enough to tip the swing structure. Many older kids had tried, just to see if it could be done, all with little success. It was a swing that was for all ages, especially older children.

I don't remember much about the swinging session that day, but I have never forgotten that brief episode that happened just before.

In my quiet moments, off and on after that, something seemed uncomfortable. Later in the fall or late summer that year, my mom followed my dad in the pick-up while he drove his tractor down to the lost ninety. I grew worried 'cause they were gone so long. I was almost in tears when mom brought him back in the truck. I'd been restless off and on ever since my road to the Damascus swing-set experience. I was to find out later what it meant.

And then, at age eight I discovered baseball. And more, I was given a different kind of revelation. I discovered grown men *got paid to play baseball.*

That was the best news I'd ever heard. Right there and then I decided I was going to be a professional baseball player. Like most everything I'd tried, I was horrible at that too, but a Walter Mitty gene must have kicked in, and my awfulness started being subdued by my dreams of how good I was *going* to be someday.

The imaginary folks I played with became a batting line-up (yes, I played on both teams … it was my fantasy, after all). Of course, I was the pitcher and would strike out the other team, and then would hit clean-up for my team.

I would toss the ball in to the air then hit it with my bat. Since I was born in '57, I didn't turn eight until November of '65, which was too late for baseball that year. However, I *was* eligible to play ball the summer of '66, and I made the most of it.

I was placed on a team named Maxwell Speed Wash. The team was named after the sponsor, a Laundromat on Leon Street in Gatesville. I was familiar with the establishment. Mom had taken me with her when our washing machine was broken and she washed our clothes there. The place had a dirt parking lot, and I imagined that we would have to practice there. I was glad when the first practice was scheduled on the playground of the school.

I was also worried that I would be one of few white boys on the team, a laughable thing to think in Gatesville, Texas in 1966. There were probably only four or five blacks in my grade, and not many more Hispanics in a class of over a hundred and twenty. I don't know why I thought that might happen; I can only guess that my impressions of professional baseball players were more influenced by the likes of the three Alou brothers in San Francisco, or Juan Marichal and Willie Mays. I knew of Koufax and Mantle and Berra, but for some reason they didn't stick with me. I am going to guess I must have seen a lot more Giants and Dodgers games on TV than Yankees, and perhaps the stars of those teams made a bigger impression on me (with the exception of Koufax).

The pennant race for my age group in Gatesville consisted of the four teams in that league. The team with the red shirts was named Miller Motor. The blue team was called Powell Supply.

But the orange team was the coolest team of all. They were called Black's Grocery. Unlike the other teams that had the same color shirt and cap. Black's had black caps with an orange B. Maxwell Speed Wash wore yellow shirts and caps. We had an M on the cap. The other teams would jeer us by saying the M stood for monkey (but maybe they were right; we were the cellar dwellers that year).

All the teams wore gray wool pants. You cannot imagine how hot wool pants in the heat of central Texas can be like. Games probably started at 8PM, with a temperature of 95 degrees and 30% humidity.

We played by professional baseball rules. There was no T-ball, or coach-pitch, or ten-run rule. Base runners were allowed to lead off. The only difference in rules was that we played six innings instead of nine. Typical scores were 35 – 21, like a football score instead of baseball. The simple reason for that was poor pitching. Eight-year-old pitchers haven't mastered the strike zone like the pro ball players. That meant there were lots of walks and lots of overthrown balls on steal attempts.

Undoubtedly, I was the worst player on the worst team. Truth be told, I may have been the worst player in the league. I was certainly one of the smallest. My congenital nystagmus made it almost impossible to judge where the ball was located.

Nystagmus is like a bad connection between the brain and the eye, and it tricks the brain into constantly making eye muscle adjustments. A person's eye moves back and forth, and it gets worse when they're excited. A fixed stationary object appears to have some movement to people who suffer from it.

Doctors have told me than if anyone who did not have nystagmus suddenly got the condition they would be extremely dizzy and would be constantly vomiting, but since I'd had it from birth, constant movement did not bother me, except for giving me a poor batting average and making me a really bad pool player.

I played right field, and in spite of my condition I got the reputation for being a hustler. I was constantly moving towards the ball every time it was hit. To others it may have looked like hustle, but the truth was I thought the ball was headed in my area every time it was in the air.

At the time of Maxwell Speed Wash no one really understood those consequences, including me. I'm glad now I didn't know; I had fun trying to improve. If someone had told me that it was impossible for me to be above average I might not have continued to play baseball. And that would have been a shame, because baseball is a wonderful game. No matter what was bothering me, when I stepped between the lines nothing mattered but the game. The object was to win, but the joy to me was the game itself. The saying: "It matters not if you win or lose, but how you play the game" was a saying I totally agreed with. I was process-oriented and I knew that how I played the game was key to winning the thing. I remember the late comic George Carlin had a comedy bit about the differences between baseball and football. He said football has a battlefield objective, but the goal of baseball is to go home. And all of us want to go home.

The coach of Maxwell was a man named Robert Ballard. He was a principal at the Gatesville State School for Boys. Mom and his wife Loyce became good friends. My dad came sometimes, but not all the time. I hated it when he didn't come, but farmers didn't have time in the summer for much of anything but harvesting crops.

I forgot to mention one other difference between professional ball players and the players in the Midget League. Mothers of pro players don't take the field and play a game against the mothers of the opposing team after their sons play. And for what it's worth, the Maxwell Speed Wash mothers went undefeated in 1966.

CHAPTER EIGHT

•

1967

School was OK that year. My teacher was Mrs. Carroll; she was a nice lady and was really tall. She seemed to have a maturity an understated elegance and a proper demeanor. She was the exact opposite of the strange sights, something new and weird that was on the horizon: hippies were making themselves known.

As the 1960's progressed, many young people were turning from mainstream Protestant religions to mystic eastern religions such as Transcendental Meditation (as championed by the exceedingly greasy-looking Maharishi Mahesh Yogi) or Zen Buddhism. Respect for authority declined among the youth, and crime rates soared to nine times the rate of the 1950's. During this time marijuana use grew enormously, even as respected figures such as Doctor Timothy Leary encouraged the use of LSD (or lysergic acid diethylamide, for the scientific among us) as a mind-opening drug.

The hippie movement endorsed drugs, rock music, mystic religions and sexual freedom, and opposed violence. Many hippies moved to Haight Ashbury in San Francisco, the East Village in New York City, or lived in communes. The rapid rise of a "New Left" applied the class perspective of Marxism to postwar America, but had little organizational connection with older Marxist organizations such as the Communist Party, and even went as far as to reject organized labor as the basis of a unified left-wing movement.

The New Left differed from the traditional left in its resistance to dogma and its emphasis on personal as well as societal change. The SDS (Students for a Democratic Society) became the organizational focus of the group and was the prime mover behind the opposition to the war in Vietnam. The Sixties left also consisted of loosely held, campus-based Trotskyist, Maoist and anarchist groups, some of which by the end of the 1960s had turned to militancy.

The overlapping, but somewhat different, movement of youth cultural radicalism was manifested by the hippies and the counter-culture. The drug sub-culture, associated with this movement, spread the recreational use of cannabis and other drugs, particularly new semi-synthetic mind-expanding drugs. The era also heralded the rejection and a reformation by hippies of traditional Christian notions on spirituality, leading to the widespread introduction of Eastern and ethnic religious thinking to western values and concepts concerning a person's religious and spiritual development. Psychedelic drugs, especially the aforementioned LSD, were popularly used medicinally, spiritually and recreationally throughout the decade, and psychedelia influenced the music, artwork and movies of the time. And if that wasn't enough, with the availability of birth control pills people started having a freer attitude towards sex, and an increase in unsafe sex as well.

This was a big year for music, with groups nobody outside their home cities had ever heard of suddenly bursting on the scene. The San Fransisco super band Jefferson Airplane released the influential *Surrealistic Pillow*. This was also the year The Velvet Underground came out with their influential self-titled debut album, *The Velvet Underground and Nico*. Also, The Doors released their self-titled debut album *The Doors* that year, and the group Love came out with their masterpiece *Forever Changes*.

The Jimi Hendrix Experience released *two* successful albums during 1967: *Are You Experienced* and *Axis: Bold as Love*. These included new innovations in guitar, trio, and recording techniques. In June of 1967 the Beatles gave birth to their seminal concept album *Sgt. Pepper's Lonely Hearts Club Band*, and then that November the Moody Blues released the album *Days of Future Passed*. And if that wasn't enough, Pink Floyd gave the rock world their debut record *The Piper at the Gates of Dawn*. The band was one of the first to play psychedelic music, an atonal mishmash featuring long instrumental solos and weird electronic effects. The goal was to sonically mimic the effects of a drug trip, and psychedelic music succeeded in spades. In December Bob Dylan released the country rock album *John Wesley Harding*. To top the decade off, the Monterey Pop Festival held in July of 1967 was to many the pinnacle of the so-called "Summer of Love".

The year also saw the birth of electronic music. The modular synthesizer (also known as the Moog, a device which had been developed in 1960 by Robert Moog and Donald Buchla), marked a major change in serious music. Innovative composers already had been experimenting with styles of electro acoustic music. Now they were able to go further with such dubious offerings as John Cage's *0'0 (Zero Silence)*, to be performed by anyone in any way; Morton Subotnik's *Silver Apples of the Moon*; and Robert Ashley's *Wolfman*.

In 1967 Alvin Lucier, one of the co-founders of the Sonic Arts Union, created "Music for a Solo Performer", in which electrodes were attached to the performer's scalp. His alpha waves, controlled by his concentration, resonated from loudspeakers, and were accompanied by occasional percussion ... and yes, I imagine it was just about as goofy as it sounds. Primitive computers were beginning used in music composition and sound synthesis, notably in Max Mathews' *Music IV* and *Music V*. By the end of the decade popular music was also using synthesizers and other electronic devices.

But for now, enough about such things. Let me tell you a little about the most important person in my life: my Dad. He was a quiet person and could barely read, but Daddy was the wisest man I ever knew. He had a temper, but only got mad at himself. He was tough and strong and calm, and let mom do the discipline; seldom was escalation up to dad. His spankings hurt a lot more than mom's, so I tried to never let things get relegated to him.

As a young adult Dad became a Christian, and got baptized in a stock tank across the road from Stanley Chapel. It must have worked, because after that he started reading his Bible all the time, and he seemed not to get mad as much. I remember his Bible was stained with oil and grease 'cause a lot of times his hands were still dirty when he picked it up. But he didn't care. That book became his life's manual. Shortly afterward joining the church he bought a recliner, and from then on, he sat in it every night and read his holy book.

When I was in the second grade I could already read out loud as well as—or maybe better than—he could. But Dad didn't feel slighted at that; it just made him prouder of me. On occasion, he would try to preach at Stanley Chapel, and when he did he stammered a lot. But that didn't seem to matter. Dad was always glad to talk about the Bible with me, or to anyone that had a question. Many people would come to our house and ask my daddy questions about it. He was always ready to give them friendly, solid, workable answers.

But one winter's day, all that changed forever.

It was Saturday morning, February 12th 1967. I recall the day as being cold, but not bitterly so; the butane heaters always made it warm inside our house. I remember watching cartoons that morning—as I always did—and playing with my pocket knife. But for some reason I started feeling bad. Restless, and ... funny inside.

My dad was in the living room putting on his black coat and preparing to go outside. For a while he watched Saturday morning cartoons with me as he put on his work boots, ready to tackle another repair job (our bull and the neighbor's bull had fought, and had torn up the fence between the two pastures). Today was the day my dad and our neighbor had agreed to meet and work on the fence together.

As he left the living room, he said to me what he always did: "See you later, horsefly."

Then he walked through the dining room and through the kitchen and out the screened in back porch down to the tractor shed.

Earlier that morning I'd gone to my parent's bedroom. My father was in the kitchen, but my mom was still in bed. Sleepily she'd reminded me that tomorrow was Dad's birthday, and asked what I wanted to get him. I really didn't know, and said as much. I left then, and my mother rolled over and went back to sleep.

Sometime later, after Daddy had left, I lost interest in the cartoons. As the morning had dragged on, the worse they'd become; it seemed the best ones were on early. As I watched, I was messing with my pocket knife. That's when I felt a sharp pain. I'd cut my finger, and it was bleeding to beat the band.

But to me it wasn't so bad; I'd been hurt worse. I woke my mom again, and she got up and administered first aid. By then my sister had awoken, and my mom made us both some oatmeal. Something was still wrong, though.

I had gone back to the living room while the oatmeal was cooking, and the heat from the butane heaters seemed to make me feel sicker than I had felt before.

About then mom called me to the kitchen table, and I obeyed. As I took my seat I stared down into my bowl of hot cereal; something about it just didn't look right. And as the minutes ticked by I began to feel worse and worse.

Suddenly, without me really knowing how it had happened, I found myself in my mother's arms, being carried through the dining room in to the living room. My mom said I had fainted and fallen backwards out of my chair, down on the kitchen floor.

By now she was very agitated, as any mother would be, at seeing her child in such a state. She made a quick phone call to the doctor and made arrangements to take me there. Then she got my little sister dressed and hurried us to the car. We backed out of the garage and pulled through our drive and started to leave.

As we rounded the house I looked toward the tractor shed, and noticed daddy's tractor and daddy sitting on it. I told mommy I wanted to tell daddy bye before we left. She wasn't looking. She said that daddy was gone, "he'd left hours ago to repair the fence." I told her no, that indeed he was right there, and I could see him.

My mom looked, and immediately I could tell that she knew something was wrong. The tractor shed was about a hundred yards away from where we were. Backing the car up, she turned us around and started towards the tractor shed. As we drew closer her voice began to change, and it became obvious even to me something was very wrong.

The tractor was stopped in the middle of the road a small ways beyond the shed, with the posthole digger that was supposed to be mounted on the back of the tractor sitting oddly above it. I could see the tractor was running but not moving and my dad was sitting lifeless on top of it, underneath the posthole digger. His face was down on the steering wheel, and a very large metallic piece of the posthole digger rested on the back of his head.

It was a surreal scene: a large green tractor, a cloudy gray sky, a black dirt road at the edge of a muddy field and at the center of it all, a lifeless black coat. And poignantly, a loyal Border collie dog setting in the road next to the tractor, waiting for his master to return from the dead, and drive the vehicle on down the road.

My mother got out of the car and stumbled over to the tractor. A moment later, shock and horror filling her face, she ran back to the car. Firing it up, we took off like a rocket.

The ride down our half-mile long country lane was very frightening. I'd never traveled so fast on that road before. When we got to the end of the lane, we turned left instead of right. My mom kept saying, "I got to get some help, I got to get some help," over and over as we flew.

We roared down the road to Andy Davidson's house, and hopefully toward aid (Andy had some teenage sons, and I'm sure Mom hoped they could help somehow). She screeched to a stop in front of their house and ran inside. Almost as instantly after she'd gone inside, she emerged again, with Andy's three teenage boys running behind her.

They got in their truck, and as fast as we'd gotten there, we returned home again. But once there, my mom didn't get out of the car. It seemed she couldn't. As much as we'd all prayed for this nightmare not to be true, nothing had changed. The green tractor and the lifeless black coat and the Border collie dog were still there, just as before.

The Davidson boys jumped out of their truck and began to pull and tug on the green contraption resting on top of my father. But it wouldn't budge. My mom cried out, "They're too little, too late!"

Heartsick and still in shock, she took Darla and me back to the house.

Time seemed to shift, and then it was like all kinds of people were there, filling the place; in a little town like ours, news such as this would travel like wildfire. Lots of people started coming over, neighbors, uncles, aunts, cousins, the doctor, a man with a wrecker, the sheriff, my Grandded.

Somewhere in this, my mother began to fall apart. She kept cradling my head and telling me, "He is resting on Abraham's bosom."

I knew who Abraham was, but I wasn't sure what a bosom was, or why my father would be resting there. I figured he was probably in heaven or at least some resting place in route to heaven.

A lot of people stared at me, as if to see how I was affected by this. Shortly after this I found out a story had gotten about that I had fainted at the sight of my dead father. Which I hadn't, of course.

The doctor came and talked to me to see if I was okay. My cousins wanted to play; maybe they were trying to get my mind off things. We got out my Fort Apache set, but somehow it wasn't much fun. Normally having everyone over to our house would have been a treat, but it wasn't. My emotions were in turmoil. In some ways having all these people around was okay, but mostly it just felt weird.

My mother continued to weep uncontrollably. As she lay on the bed, she would repeatedly send for me and ask if I was okay. She apologized for scaring me and my sister when she drove the car for help. To this day I have not forgotten how the sumac tree on the side of the road came and passed by so quickly, and the roar of the dirt and rocks being thrown up against the car as we raced down the narrow lane.

There may have been a half-dozen people with my mother as she cried without solace on her bed of pain. The doctor came to the house again, but Mom refused to take any medication; why, I don't know.

By then there were dozens of people all over our house, and most of them remained until late. Some stayed all night, while the rest came back the next day. I recall they brought what seemed like tons food and they made gallons of coffee and they were simply *everywhere*. They even fed our cows and took care of the farm.

My Aunt Wanda and I were in the kitchen when she turned to me and said, "Well, I guess you're the man of the house now." Those words seemed totally alien to my ears, yet I believed they were true. From that point on, I never cried in front of anyone and never really let go until I was twenty-three, fourteen years later.

From the other room, I then began to hear people whispering. They were going on about how Daddy had died. I know I wasn't meant to hear it, but stung just the same. They said the posthole digger had killed Daddy instantly when it landed on his head (the digger was not made for that tractor, and my dad had fabricated it to fit). They said allegedly it was riding too low in its cradle, and hit a rock while he was driving. The rock then forced the bottom of the digger up, and the top of it lanced forward toward the tractor seat.

And that was it.

— • —

I remember the funeral; it was sad, scary and I found it almost impossible to breathe. At the time of this writing I was fifty years old, and had many trials and tribulations. But none of them had ever been as hard as putting my father to rest.

Sitting on the front row near my mother, I looked at the casket with Daddy laying there. As my mother bawled uncontrollably, the sound was almost enough to suck the very life out of me. It was like there were heavy bricks on my chest, and it seemed to be a burden to just to inhale and exhale.

But as I said, I didn't shed a tear. I recall at some point either before or after the funeral my mom encouraging me to cry, saying it would help, but I couldn't. The gates of hell itself could not unleash any moisture from my eyes. In my young mind, it was now my duty to be the man of the family and I could not and would not cry. To do so would be a betrayal to my father and my mother and my sister.

And I had to be strong; my mother was crying enough to wash out the sun and my sister was too little to even know what was happening. Somehow, I got through that awful day and grew up and learned to cry, and the scars healed. So I thought.

One day when I was in my forties, I was building fence. The sun was warm, and I removed my black coat and hung it on a fence post. As I worked my way down the fence line, I turned.

And my heart nearly stopped in my chest at the sight of my lifeless black coat hanging there. Just like my dad's coat had been that terrible day. As jolting as that picture was, I was even more shocked at how it still affected me, then and now. I have a Dodge extended cab pickup, and when the seat is released forward and is resting up against the steering wheel, I think of it as being in the "dead man position," and that bothers me.

But there is a lot more good I learned from my dad that outweighs the burden of the lifeless black coat.

Everybody liked Daddy, and when he died the funeral home pews were full. Matter of fact the whole building was packed tight. There was no place to stand inside, and the yard outside of the funeral home was full of people standing as well. My Great-Uncle Bill Kays said the yard was so full of people that he had to stand on the curb next to the street. They ended up having to put speakers outside so people standing outside could hear. The funeral director said he had buried rich and poor, and never had seen so many people show up at a funeral.

After my father's home going, things changed. We moved in with my mom's parents until the end of the school year. We would go home occasionally, but not for very long. Lloyd Cathey came and got Old Betty. I really couldn't squawk much; it was his horse anyway.

In reality, I guess I was too shocked about everything else to even care about the horse. It never dawned on me that my whole lifestyle was about to change. My uncle rounded up all the cows and sold them at the cattle auction. A relative or a neighbor wanted the bull and he was sold separately without going to auction.

And things at home were growing tense. Uncle Ray and Grandded were telling my mom what to do on just about every turn. My mom would struggle with every decision but would eventually come around to their way of thinking. It wasn't that she first opposed what they said, she was just indecisive.

No one knew much about mental health back then; for that matter, I'm not sure people know much about it now. But they sure didn't know much back then. At any rate,

I know now my mom was in a depression. It lasted for years and influenced me greatly, probably more than I even realize.

One day a sharp-dressed man with an easy smile came over and talked to Uncle Ray and Grandded and then talked to my mom and Uncle Ray and Grandded all together. He was an auctioneer, and said he'd be handling the Whisenhunt auction. He then said we could make even more money if we sold food during the sale. His big mistake was suggesting that my sister and I could sell lemonade there.

At that my mom put her foot down and said her children would not be "food hawkers" as their father's possessions were being sold.

The day of the auction I sat on the swing and watched farm implements leave one by one as they were hauled from the tractor shed, past the house and down the driveway, never to be seen again. The adults were interested in the sale of the three tractors, but the old grain trucks were the most noteworthy to me. In my early years, they served as play ground equipment. After all, a young boy is part monkey, and crawling all over a grain truck is an irresistible challenge. Sir Edmund Hillary had Mt. Everest; I had grain trucks and windmills to climb. The windmills were listed as off limits 'cause those blades at the top could send you crashing to the ground. But a grain truck was seldom forbidden. On a hot day in the field, one could find a shady refuge underneath a big old grain truck. If the afternoon got really scorching, the metal could get hot enough to fry an egg, and since it would be foolish to climb on a cook stove, boys in Texas would refrain from walking around barefooted on a grain truck in the middle of the summer. But you might find those same boys playing in the dirt in the shade underneath one of these oversized automobiles.

When I was a baby, one of our old trucks had a rusted-out floorboard. The hole was big enough for one of my plastic toy horses to fit through. As my mom and I had set in the fields waiting on my father to swing by on the combine to unload wheat or maize, I'd make a game of trying to throw my toy horse through the hole in the floorboard (when one's bored, you have to use your imagination to come up with something to do; this game was as good as any). If the toy fell through the hole, then you had an excuse to get out of the truck and crawl underneath it to retrieve the plastic stallion that had escaped.

The day of the auction, as the old pieces of junk rumbled past the house, I jumped out of the swing and said something to myself about "the trucks leaving, the trucks leaving." Like a plug removed from a bathtub, the things that had surrounded my life for years were draining away, one by one.

I really didn't comprehend what was going on. It was probably a good thing for me that most of this was over my head; I guess the good Lord was watching out for me, even then.

My grandparents had built a new house on a forty-acre cedar brake in northern Coryell County between Turnersville and Clifton, and this is where my mom and sister and I lived after the funeral. Grandded was fifty-five and Grandma was fifty-four, and this was the first house they'd ever owned. Until that time, they'd always rented or leased.

These days we think we're entitled to buy a home as soon as we get married, if not before. In the Sixties, home ownership was not a certainty. My grandparents had raised five kids through the great depression and watched WWII and the Korean conflict come and go, and finally after years of scratching the ground and scraping their dimes together, they bought a forty-acre pile of rocks crowned with a thicket so dense a goat couldn't walk through it.

Grandded bulldozed it, burned it, fenced it and built a house. It was brick, built on a pier and beam foundation, with a one-car port and a laundry room. It had central heat, and as most houses do it had an indoor bathroom that actually had a bathtub and shower head. It was pretty modern by my standards; it even had carpet in the living room and in the three bedrooms.

My grandparents got up at 5:00 AM, and promptly served breakfast at 5:30 every morning. Any house guest had to be at the table at 5:30, no exceptions. At that young age, I remember how eerie it looked out the window just before dawn. The morning fog was laced with smoke from some of the huge brush piles that were smoldering.

The goats were scattered here and there, and sometimes stood on their hind legs to reach a leaf they wanted to eat. When they stood like that, to my little-boy eyes it was as though men were standing there in the shimmering haze. Sleepiness, coupled with the morning fog and the smoke and the nimble animals outside fused nicely with my vivid imagination. I asked my grandma who were those people standing out in the pasture.

Besides being some place other than home under difficult circumstances, living in my grandparents' house was not an easy change. I'm not talking about the crazy hour for breakfast, now; I'm talking about the house's heat.

The central heat there blew loud and blew hot. I was used to warm rooms when the butane heaters were on during the day, but not at night. It sounds strange, but if one is used to sleeping under a sheet, a blanket and three quilts, and being able to see their breath because of the cold, they don't like hot air blowing on them … not to mention the whooshing sound of the furnace turning on. My mom and I had actually thought we would enjoy being in a new warm house. We were surprised at our on disappointment.

Looking back, I don't think her ongoing dissatisfaction had anything to do with her depression; it had everything to do with what we were used to and personal preferences. Change can be difficult. You may be thinking "bull corn," at that (okay, maybe corn isn't what you would have said after "bull"). Anyway, you'd think if my grandparents liked it, their house must not have been that bad. They had to like it; it was their house.

For instance, my Grandded found what he thought was a good deal on some pipe for his water well (in reality, it was some old pipe from an oil well). It turned out not to be such a great idea. The pipe made the water stink so badly it was undrinkable for over a year, and barely suitable for bathing.

But my Grandded was undeterred. You should have heard him try to downplay the condition of the water. I can't count how many times I heard him talk about how he used to drink water out of a muddy cow track when he was boy. I'm sure they were proud of their house, but I also know that no house, even a dream house, is ever perfect.

As the year dragged on, my father's mortality made me wonder about my own. Maybe it was related to that, but shortly after we stayed at my grandparents, my right arm broke out in boils and became swollen and was hot. The doctor said I had a virus there. He told my mom to wrap my arm in raw bacon to pull the poison out. As a nine-year-old I often wondered when I was going to die. We were studying health in school, and I began to worry about what part of my body was going to do me in.

Here's something weird: I got where I was afraid to swallow. I was afraid I would swallow my tongue or my epiglottis. My Grandded almost had a wall-eyed fit at that. I guess a man who felt comfortable drinking from a muddy cow track had no tolerance for a pint size hypochondriac like me. My phobias subsided after a week or so, much to the relief of everyone in the house.

When summer came, my mom, my sister and I went to west Texas. My dad's sister and her husband lived in a town called Crane, which wasn't far from Odessa and Midland.

Aunt Ruberta and Uncle Morris were glad to see us. Uncle Morris was pretty high up with Gulf Oil Company, and he got my mom a series of job interviews there (she'd been trying for a while now after Dad's death to get a job). She didn't get one.

Years later I learned that she would have gotten the job if she'd acted like she wanted it. Mom was really smart and had worked for the Federal Reserve in Dallas before she was married.

After things fell through at Gulf Oil, Mom decided to stay in central Texas and take her chances finding something else there. I remember being dragged around Waco as she took civil service tests for the Post Office and other places.

Finally, she landed a position working for the Coryell County Farm Bureau. My mom's sister, Berta Mae then came to stay with us for the summer (she was to watch us while mom was at work). My mom tried to warn my sister and me that Berta Mae was gonna take a little getting used to. She kept saying that Berta Mae didn't have any kids, but she had a lotta ideas about raising kids. She told us to be nice to her, even if she came up with something we didn't think very much of.

Poor old Aunt Berta Mae discovered her theories didn't do so well in a real world application. The more she bullyragged me, the more I got plum muley stubborn, even more so after she poured water on me to get me outta bed at 10 o'clock in the morning.

It just wasn't fair. I'd spent the last three months or so being waked up at 5:30 in the morning by my grandmother. Now school was out for summer, and I was back at my house in my own bed, and to my thinking as long as I got up in time for lunch, nobody should care. Things got heated for a while. My aunt couldn't get me to do anything, and I didn't care. I was gonna show her that she couldn't make me. My sister followed suit. At the end Mom had to tell all of us to back off, including Aunt Berta Mae. That summer was a pretty bumpy one, but we got through it somehow.

I can't remember what happened when school started back. I guess mom took us to school on her way to work.

CHAPTER NINE

LATE 1967 TO EARLY 1968

My teacher that year was Mrs. Stiles, a real taskmaster. She was from Ater and knew my Grandparents, and so held me to a higher standard than anyone else. She blamed me once when the flag got hung upside down, even though I was not the leader of the four-person squad responsible for hanging the thing. I'd told the other three I thought it was upside down, but nobody listened. When the high school called and asked why we were signaling for distress, Mrs. Stiles chewed me out. Life just wasn't fair.

But then some girls started wearing fish net stockings that year—and I noticed—so maybe it was fairer than I thought. It was not until my sophomore year that I even remember girls wearing jeans or pants to school. They went from miniskirts to jeans over the summer of '73; Gatesville may have been behind the rest of the country.

This was the year Johnny Cash released *At Folsom Prison* with the monster hit single, *A Boy Named Sue*... and with that I'd like to address something near and dear to my heart:

country music. Contrary to popular belief, in the Sixties everybody wasn't a stoned hippie, and for sure everybody didn't go to Woodstock. There was a huge amount of country music getting airplay, and in the Whisenhunt house we heard a lot of it. In the Sixties I listened to what my parents listened to, but even then there was a bit of friction. I liked Roger Miller but my parents didn't (Buck Owens I also liked). In the late Fifties and early Sixties on my mom's kitchen radio we listened to such country tunes as *Second Fiddle, Under Your Spell Again, Foolin' Around,* and *Nobody's Fool but Yours.*

In the mid-sixties, it was songs like *Act Naturally* (later redone in 1989 by Ringo Starr, of all people), *Think of Me, I've Got a Tiger by the Tail,* and *Buckeroo* (maybe named after Buck Owens and his Buckaroos; I don't know). And from the mid-Sixties to the end of the decade our family enjoyed hearing such country favorites as *Sam's Place, Sweet Rosie Jones, I've Got You on My Mind Again,* and *Who's Gonna Mow Your Grass.*

On the rock scene, 1968 was huge. The Rolling Stones filmed the TV special *Rock and Roll Circus* in December of that year, a concert which oddly was never broadcast during its contemporary time. Considered for decades as a fabled "lost" performance, it remained that way until it was discovered and released in North America on Laserdisc and VHS in 1995. The concert showcased performances from The Who, The Dirty Mac (featuring John Lennon, Eric Clapton and Mitch Mitchell), Jethro Tull, and Taj Mahal.

After The Yardbirds had folded, guitarist Jimmy Page and manager Peter Grant met with vocalist Robert Plant, who together with drummer John Bonham and bassman John Paul Jones formed a new group, calling themselves Led Zeppelin. That year they released their début album by the same name. In 1968 the seminal group simply calling themselves The Band also released the root album *Music from Big Pink.*

Big Brother and the Holding Company, with Janis Joplin as lead singer, had become an overnight sensation after their performance at Monterey Pop in 1967, and the following year released their massively successful second album *Cheap Thrills* with its monster single, *Piece of my Heart.* Also in 1968, The Jimi Hendrix Experience released the highly influential double LP *Electric Ladyland,* a set that furthered the guitar and studio innovations of the previous two albums.

Music was the theme of change, and all across America a huge movement was now rising in opposition to the Vietnam War, an opposition which for all intents and purposes came to its peak in the massive Moratorium protests in 1969.

By mid-1968 things had gotten worse for the Johnson administration. Late in January of that year the DRV (or North Vietnamese) and the NFL (*not* the football guys) had begun to attack some major cities in South Vietnam. The attacks were known as the Tet Offensive, and were a way to force the Johnson administration to the bargaining table.

By now Americans in general were getting war-weary—as the Communist Party correctly predicted—and a lot of folks figured we weren't likely to succeed much longer in the war. Many people thought that the Tet Offensive was a military defeat, and that thinking produced the desired result: Lyndon Johnson was disgraced. Blamed by many for the war and the racial unrest in the country, he did not run for reelection in 1968, announcing he would not seek the Democratic Party's re-nomination for president. But he then hinted he was going to the bargaining table to end the war.

A part of the anti-war movement consisted of resistance to conscription ("the draft") for the war. Of course, we rural folks fought this madness with everything we had, our counterpunches being summed up in songs by Merle Haggard like "The Fightin' Side of Me" and "Okie from Muskogee," country hits which topped the charts.

Historically the antiwar movement was initially based on the older 1950s peace movement (which had been heavily influenced by the American Communist Party), but by the mid-1960s it outgrew this and became a broad-based mass movement centered on the universities and churches. One kind of protest was called a *"sit-in,"* which is exactly like it sounds. On a given day the protestors would sit in front of Army recruiting centers, munitions factories, chemical plants, you name it, and when the cops would show up to haul them away the protestors would go as limp as noodles, to make it that much harder to remove them (anybody who's even tried to lift up a toddler who doesn't want to go to the doctor knows just how tough it is to move dead weight).

Other terms heard nationally included *draft dodger, conscientious objector,* and *Vietnam vet.* Voter age-limits were challenged by the phrase: "If you're old enough to die for your country, you're old enough to vote." Many of the youth involved in the politics of the movements distanced themselves from the "hippies"—they were the more serious protesters with a real cause.

And it got progressively worse. On May 4, 1970, the growing anti-war demonstrations came to a bloody culmination with the Kent State shootings. By that year university students were protesting the war and the draft in earnest. Riots had ensued during that previous weekend and the National Guard was called into maintain the peace.
However, by Monday tensions arose again, and as the crowd grew larger, the guardsmen started shooting. When it was over four students were dead and nine injured. This event caused disbelief and shock throughout the country, and became a staple of further anti-Vietnam demonstrations.

But by mid-1967 that event was still three years off, and war and protests and politics and civil rights had all taken second place in my mind. My father's death had interrupted everything in my young life. Even my restlessness was interrupted. My mom could not stand to go back to Stanley Chapel to attend worship services. She said there were just too many memories, saying she could see my father still standing in the pulpit. That seemed strange to me since he really didn't stand in the pulpit very often. Before my dad died, there had been talk about a church in town that had a really good preacher. I think my dad went and heard him preach one time. Someone suggested we try visiting it.

The preacher there was a little man named Roland McLean. He was probably just barely five feet tall, bald-headed, and always sporting an ear to ear grin. You could tell he had a heart much bigger than he was. He didn't preach hell fire and brimstone like all the paid preachers I had heard before, although I knew a lot of people who never spoke kindly of paid preachers. They said they were lazy and should carry their own weight.

My daddy had said he didn't see anything wrong with paid preachers. He told us there was a verse in the Bible that said not to muzzle the ox that treads the grain. I had no idea what an ox treading grain had to do with a man getting paid to stand up in front of people and preach. Mom explained that preaching was like treading grain, and if an ox gets to eat the grain while he is working, then a preacher ought to get paid for preaching.

As usual, mom was the one who explained stuff. Daddy said stuff, but mom was the one that explained it. Mom was used to quoting ideas that daddy used to say and then explaining what it meant. For instance, my dad once had said that Billy Graham was a good preacher, but he stopped his sermons before he got to the end. Mom said that meant that Billy was a Baptist, but he really didn't believe in baptism.

Before I go any further, I don't intend to ruffle the feathers of my Baptists friends, and trust me I've heard all the arguments, pro and con. I'd been called a Campbellite, and heard and read about salvation through faith, and not through works, and listened to arguments on whether or not baptism is a work. I'm sure now I could preach a sermon on either side of the issue. I don't think baptism is a work, but this book isn't meant to be a dissertation on salvation, or sacraments, or any of that. But from a historical perspective, this topic was a very big deal in the 1960's in the denominations I was around.

When we attended Brother McLean's church, I was pleasantly surprised. I'd never been in a church before that had air conditioning. Plus, the floor didn't squeak when you walked on it … always a bonus. It didn't have any windows to speak of, and there weren't really any distractions in the auditorium during services.

In addition, this church had a baptistery inside the building. I had never heard or seen such a thing. Everybody I knew had gotten baptized outside in a stock tank (most of the rest of America would call it a pond, but where I was from it was called a tank). I had heard of people getting baptized in a river, but I don't think I ever saw anyone get baptized in one. The reason was simple. Many of the river banks where I grew up were covered in poison ivy and tall grass and weeds that made it kind of snaky. Most people preferred a stock tank; truth be told, many people back then in our town couldn't swim. Matter of fact, I didn't learn to swim until I was an adult; I taught myself at night after the pool where I was living was closed. I was afraid that if I drowned when people were around, I'd be embarrassed. I'm serious.

Anyway, not only did this church have a baptistery, but they had a mural on the wall behind it to make it look like it was in a river (I think it was supposed to be the Jordan River). The quality of the artwork wasn't that good, but it was impressive to me just the same. They even had a curtain to cover it up so people wouldn't get distracted when the preacher was preaching. There was also a sheet of thick glass between the curtain and the water to keep people from falling into the water. All in all, this was the fanciest church I had ever seen in my life. Looking back now, I realize that this was a very Spartan building; very plain by almost any standards except for Stanley Chapel. I guess my head would have exploded if I had gone to the Sistine Chapel or even any Catholic Church back then.

Things at the Whisenhunt place were getting back to almost normal. Roland McLean talked to my mom a few times, and she had him come to our house to talk to me. Someone once said that I had an inferiority complex. Probably because of my "twin tower" issues. The truth is that was only half the story. The other half took therapy as an adult to discover. Something more people should probably try.

When Reverend McLean asked me if anything was bothering me, I told him that I had an inferiority complex, as opposed to being a mean arrogant kid (I really didn't know any mean arrogant kids, but it sounded good). The preacher wisely told me that it didn't matter if one had a superiority complex or an inferiority complex. I asked for an explanation. He said both were selfish thinking.

He said thinking good about yourself or thinking bad about yourself was still thinking about yourself. He said one should think about God and others and not think about themselves. It was profound and profoundly simple.

I don't know if you believe in coincidences, but I got baptized a few months later on November 11th, 1967. It was my mom and dad's wedding anniversary. I have heard that there are no such things as coincidences, that providence is mistaken for coincidence. That day I became a Christian, and unbeknownst to me perhaps that was an anniversary gift to my dad in heaven, and my mom on earth.

The night I stepped forward, I didn't even realize it was their anniversary. I did realize it was Veteran's Day. Strangely the sermon that night was on marriage. I whispered to my mom if it was appropriate to step forward, even though the sermon did not apply to me, or my situation. She said it was not a problem. So I did, and I've never been the same. Sure, I am not perfect, but Jesus is my Savior. Just thought of something, if I had a broken arm while I was being baptized, it would still have been broken when I came out of the water. Sins may be washed away but wounds seen and unseen often take time to heal.

But back to more mundane matters. There was growing talk that Mrs. Alvis would only let us live in the house we rented from her for the rest of the year (she had let us stay there since February). No one would blame her; Mrs. Alvis owned all this land and needed someone to work it, and she was doubtful of finding someone to do that without renting the house too. It was her property, and property was the way she made a living. She was old, and leases and rents were her income. Her husband was deceased. He had been a partner with others in a couple of department stores.

Mom began looking for a house in town (Gatesville) then. After my dad's death, she still had some cash from the auction. We looked at a nice brick house on a street name I can't remember, although I could drive right to it to this very day; I went to a birthday party of a boy on my baseball team not far from that house. Mom was worried about the septic tank so she didn't buy it.

A lot of children lived on Jackson Drive and on 28th Street. Mom had complained about kids playing in the street. It probably seems perfectly normal to you, but we had a strong sense of property rights and a desire to not be somewhere you weren't supposed to be. We thought children should play in yards and not in streets where cars drive. She looked at a house a few blocks over on Mears Drive but she decided against that one too.

She finally ended up buying a house from Burney Baize on the east side of town near the Highway Department (that's what Texas used to call the Department of Transportation in the Sixties), and across the highway from Lion's Field (the local baseball field for ages ten and up). Burney was moving to a farm near Crawford, the future home of President George W. Bush. No, I don't mean that the President bought Burney's farm, I mean the Bush's and the Baize's both lived near Crawford. Although, I've long suspected the President's place is probably closer to Osage or Coryell City than it is to Crawford. I have never driven past the Bush place so I'm not certain, but I digress.

That day a bunch of my relatives came and helped us move off the Alvis place to the three bedroom, one-and-a-half bath red brick house on Royal Drive. And for some reason I couldn't get the crazy thought out of my head that I had to live in town because I was no longer good enough to live in the country.

The weather had been typical December weather in Texas. That means to most a warm spring day. Let me tell you a little bit about our weather. Texas has four seasons: winter, which runs from Jan 1st to February 21st, followed by summer, which lasts from around the 1st of March until the 1st of June (this is followed by Texas summer, a season that every year lasts from June until October). This is then followed by Indian summer, and that lasts from October until the end of the year.

Now there is the occasional cold snap that typically lasts for only three days or so, and when it comes it falls anytime between October and December, or during March and April. Texas can and has had droughts and floods in the same year, and that statistically shows as having a normal year.

Of course, the surest way to make it rain is to wash your car or plan to move all your belongings in open air grain trucks and cattle trailers. And we found that out when we got the rain and a cold snap the day we moved. One of my mom's favorite quilts blew partly out of one of the trucks driven by Uncle Ray. It was dragged in the rain and the wet streets the nine miles or so from the Alvis place through Gatesville and to our new home about a mile east of town. If you'll bear with me for a moment, I'd like to describe that house. Mentally I was still going through a lot for a boy, and those memories of that dwelling are still as sharp as the smell of acetone.

The house had a front door facing south on a small porch, and the garage also faced south and towards the street on the west side of it. The back door faced east on the north side of the house. The back door, which was in the kitchen, opened to a small patio. South of the kitchen was the den; along the west wall there was a third door that opened into the garage.

The garage was double-car width, with a double-sized door on the south, facing the street, and a single garage door on the north side. This allowed one to drive through the garage into the backyard. From the den one could walk through a sliding door on the east wall near the front door, into the front entry way. Across from the front door on the north side of the entry way was an opening to a living room. The living room had a small chandelier and a large window that consumed almost the entire north wall and looked out across the patio in to the backyard. East of the front entry there was a long hall that led to the bedrooms. My bedroom was the first one on the right facing south toward the street.

When entering this bedroom, the closet was on the left, and the majority of the bedroom was to the right of the hallway door. At the end of the hall was my sister's bedroom, which was on the right, on the southeast corner of the house. The majority of her room was to the left of the hallway door and her closet was on the right sharing the same wall as my closet but closer to the street than mine. Her room had two sets of windows facing the street on the south and another set of windows on the east. All of the windows in the house were high and the cross ventilation was poorer than our house in the country.

The ceilings were only eight feet high; two feet lower than the house on the Alvis place. The advantage was the house was warmer in the winter but the disadvantage was that it was warmer in the summer as well. At the end of the hall, the hall turned north and the bathroom was on the right on the east side of the house. North of the bathroom was my mom's bedroom on the northeast side of the house. It was the coolest bedroom in the summer and winter. It had double windows on the east and the north walls.

On the northwest side of the bedroom there was a small bathroom with a built-in shower, but no bath. As you may surmise the majority of this master bathroom was on the right side of the door as you entered the room. A door to a walk-in closet was on the left when you walked in to the room, and the door to the master half bath was also on the left. The house was built on a concrete slab, with linoleum tile glued down to the foundation in every room except the living room; that one had carpet. Gone were the hardwood floors of the old place.

The new house had an electric furnace and the door to its closet was across the hall from my bedroom door. We had to run the furnace the very first night. It was nicer than those old butane heaters that we had before, except the electric heat blew air set at 70 to 80 degrees from the duct work in the ceiling.

The air that blew from it felt cool to the skin, and gone was the warmth of the open flame of the Dearborn stoves that had been placed in each room of the old house. I still liked it better than the hot air that blew from the gas furnace from Grandded's new house that I spoke of earlier. Gas is more efficient, but I knew nothing of that then.

The new house had been built with a hip roof construction on all four sides with no gables, just as the old house. But it looked very different. The old house was more squarely built, with the garage a separate square tied in near one corner. The new house was more distinctly a rectangle with the garage part of that rectangle.

Another similarity was although the heating solution was different, neither had any air conditioning. The old house accommodated for the oppressive Texas heat quite nicely with the high ceilings, pier and beam construction, and lots of windows looking out on an open prairie. The new house had almost none of the architectural features that were necessary to keep the heat down inside in the summer time. The house was situated in a cedar break, and the wind did not blow well as it did on the open prairie.

Our new place was situated on a lot of seventy feet wide by one hundred ten feet deep. Royal Drive was only one block long, and only one block off Highway 84, the major road to Waco. There were seven houses on our street. Our house was on the center, and had two or three vacant lots between it and the closest house on the same side of the street.

There was a house directly across from us owned by a wealthy rancher who decided to raise his family in town. We were not actually in the city limits but certainly close enough.

Walking the yard took less time than it took to walk to the barn on the Alvis place. I thought it was wrong to step one foot beyond the property line. I had never once dared to trespass on the land farmed by Mr. Davidson, or Mr. Necessary, or crossed across where Henry Lengefield had lived or even placed a toe on the land owned by Horace Jackson or Mr. Schloeman. Of course, I was setting on close to six hundred acres before. The transition to a lot of seventy by one hundred ten feet was like still being inside the house.

We had some nice trees to climb in the front yard. There was an oak by the street with a first limb was at least seven feet off the ground, but it had some adequate toe holds on the trunk. My sister and I taught the other kids on the street how to climb it as the years passed by. In the front yard by the porch there was a large cedar that an adult could barely get their arms around. It was struck by lightning the first year we lived there and Uncle Dale cut it down, leaving a stump just under three feet high.

I remember sparks flying off the chain saw when he tried to cut that tree; the wood was just that tough. He said he was going to get rid of the whole thing, but after such a battle to cut it down, he decided to leave the stump. That stump became a magnet for children to sit on in the front yard. All of the flower beds on the east and north side of the house were planted in castor beans that were as tall as the eve of the house.

Mom, being the natural worry-wart, did not like having a poisonous plant in the yard (maybe she thought we'd accidentally eat them), so that first year she and I eradicated those large plants and their seedlings. I was quite adept at using a hoe from the hours chopping Johnson grass in the cotton patch; but the sifted soil I'd been used to was not here. The dirt around the new house consisted of some hard clay trucked in for the construction of the foundation. It was almost like striking the concrete foundation itself.

To my thinking it was easier to spend two hours in a cotton patch than ten minutes in these so-called flower beds. After we got rid of those blasted plants, I had to dig holes and plant bulbs. Most of them didn't come up. It seemed our green thumbs from the Alvis place hadn't followed us to Royal Drive.

But eventually we did get our green thumbs back and managed to get some Easter Lilies to come up, and they did quite nicely. We also put in a banana plant in a sheltered flower bed next to the garage and the front porch. It yearly took quite a beating from rebounded basketballs falling on in it and from the occasional cold snaps in the winter time.

But just as the legendary phoenix rises up from the ashes, each spring it would resurrect from the brown dead leaves and trunk that had fallen to the ground. It would then become a four and half to six feet tall plant throughout the summer, thriving in good health like that, only to suffer abuse and cold another year when winter came calling. Aggravatingly enough, it never grew any bananas; I guess we were too far north.

One day I suffered quite a start from it when an errant baseball rolled under the green plant. The leaves were drooping low to the ground, and I fell to the turf and extended my hand out beneath the thing to retrieve the ball.

That's when my fingers grasped something cold and clammy.

Immediately I let go with a shudder, and then started making as much distance—both horizontally and vertically—as possible between me and the whatever-it-was. But who was I fooling? I knew full well what it was I had grabbed: a snake, and a quite thick one at that. But I just had to see it. As soon as I could get up the nerve, I lifted the leaf up to sneak a peek.

Only to find a large frog placidly looking back at me.

CHAPTER TEN

◆

1968

I have told of several deaths throughout this book. I am now going to tell about another one: the death of our television. My mom and dad had bought a black and white Magnavox television before I was born; by 1967 it was at least ten years old and we had to have the TV repair man come to the house several times to replace the vacuum tubes. By the way, I think I know where people got the idea about striking the side of something to make it work. It used to work sometimes when vacuum tube connections were loose, or when the filaments in the tube were making intermittent contact. That said, I *strongly* discourage striking the side of today's electronics. Trust me, the inside of today's stuff is a lot different than the inside of gear back then. I guess the evolution of electronics and electronic appliances could be a book in and of itself.

Anyway, all that jostling and vibration and temperature changes it had endured hadn't done the old set any good, and I guess it being rained on during the move was the final straw for our old Magnavox. It completely gave up the ghost a few weeks after we were there. This time when the TV guy came out, he told my mom it was beyond repair. She sadly replied she didn't have enough money to buy a new one.

But then her sister Berta Mae came to the rescue. She told us she had a small nineteen-inch black and white TV she no longer wanted, and said we could use it. Of course, we jumped at the offer. When it arrived, we found it came with its own stand with wheels, and was designed to have a modern look to it; funny now to think that a black and white TV could ever be considered modern. Our old set had been like a piece of furniture. It sat on wooden legs, and was enclosed in a wooden cavity with the glass protruding slightly out the front, and the knobs situated in a recessed area on the top.

The TV we got from Aunt Berta Mae had a metal chassis, and was done up in a two-tone paint job (the tones were a kind of a pinkish orange and beige; odd, to say the least). On the top it had a set of rabbit ear antennas that telescoped out; you older folks will remember those. It was a lot smaller than our old TV. And did I mention that Aunt Berta Mae's TV was also old? No wonder she no longer wanted it … and for good reason.

I'm not sure if the rabbit ears added to the problem, but we discovered the reception we got on it was not very good. We experimented by positioning the antennas, and moving the television to different parts of the house; none of it really helped. Matter of fact you had to hold your mouth right to get it to work, and that's the gospel truth. We tried slapping the side of the metal chassis, jiggling it, and every other conceivable thing on earth to get a decent picture.

Through trial and error, we finally found out the secret formula to get the best picture was to have the TV lean to its right a few degrees. To keep it there we then stuck a small spool of thread underneath the left side of the set, and presto, we had a somewhat viewable image to look at. And that spool of thread was crucial; if it was removed and the TV sat level, all we got was static and snow. But place the spool back and once again we could enjoy a picture (albeit a little fuzzy).

It was on this set that I watched the first man walk on the moon. I think it was Walter Cronkite reporting as he watched the same images that the rest of America was watching. He commented about the fuzziness of some of the images, but I couldn't really tell because everything on our set was always fuzzy. Some days were worse than others, but that night the picture seemed significantly ghostlike. They blamed it on the great distance that the signal was being transmitted from the moon to the earth. If only the astronauts had had a spool of thread …

Mrs. King was my teacher that year. She was okay, but she wasn't as interesting as my home room teacher the following year, the math instructor Mrs. Huntley. I say that because she once shot a deer from her back porch … and how many teachers did you have that did *that?*

There was a tomboy girl in Mrs. King's class, and we talked to each other, which was great; I had not spent much time talking to girls before. Anyway, while the tomboy girl and I were never boy friend/girl friend, I noticed girls could be interesting. Up until then if you liked one, or vice versa, you chunked rocks at each other, or played chase. Now it came to me there might be better things that we could do together.

I can't remember if Robert Ballard was my coach the second year I played for Maxwell Speed Wash, which was in the summer of '67. I know he wasn't my coach when I played for K&N Root Beer in the summer of '68. I also know that after Dad died that Mom used to take my sister and me over to visit at their house.

The Ballards lived in a rock house alongside highway 36, halfway between Gatesville and Jonesboro, just past the turnoff for Turnersville and Hay Valley, and then past a dip in the road known by the men at the Highway Department as Yows Draw (I learned so when I worked for the Highway Department after high school). There was a turnoff on the left or south side of the highway, and the Ballard home was on the right. Mom said this was a place called Ames.

The countryside where I grew up is so interesting; every place seems to have a name. One almost has to be a historian to appreciate all the names for some of the most subtle geographic features. My mom's mother's parents had lived around Ames when my grandmother was a young girl. The wolf and horse story told earlier happened there.

Another interesting thing about places in the country is that many of them almost seem to be an idea, instead of a real exact location.

My great-grandparents did not live near the location of the Ballard home, but a few miles south of the rock house. The dirt road across from the Ballard's led south towards the Leon River, and closer to where my great-grandparents once lived. North of the highway and northwest of the rock house is where many, many years ago a Swede lived in a dwelling on a sled.

He was a shepherd, and supposedly a real character. He refused to carry a gun, and would constantly move his house with a team of mules to follow his sheep herd. The local cattlemen would beat him, but would not kill him in a gun battle because he had no gun and they knew they would be charged for murder if they shot him (they could not claim self defense if they shot a man with no gun). Grandded used to tell me this story; I guess he learned it from someone else when he was a boy.

I mentioned earlier that Robert worked as a principal at the State School. He also raised hogs. He had several hutches and various barns and sheds on the property. The Ballard family had three boys and one girl, and they were a bit younger than me. My mom grew real close to Loyce, the wife and mother of the household. There was a neighbor across the highway that lived in the first house on the left down the dirt road. My mom became friends with them too.

Their last name was Knoll, and we occasionally visited their house. Linda and Alfred were their first names. I'd heard that Alfred had cancer, but we never talked about it around them. They were a young family, much younger than my mom, and they had a very young daughter. My mom worked at Farm Bureau Insurance, and the Knolls had their car insurance there. One time after work she came home amused, regarding a series of unfortunate events that concerned the Knoll family.

It seemed there was a horse on their place (I am not sure if it was their horse; I think they only rented the house and the land was worked by someone else) that had escaped the pasture. Anyway, once he was out the horse decided to scrape some of the paint off of their car with his teeth (yes, horses can and do such things).

The insurance agent came out and took pictures of the car with a Polaroid camera (my mom often got tickled when these town guys in suits went out on a farm; they were so bumbling and ineffectual). This visit proved to be no different. I don't remember if the Knoll's insurance policy covered the car getting the paint eaten by the horse, but the insurance company had to pay for the horse when it died from eating the developer paper that the agent had thrown on the ground.

Alfred liked to work with wood. Once after he had gotten out of the hospital, he went out to his shop and made a small stool with a place underneath to store magazines. Then he gave it to my mom.

That made a big impression on me. I'm sure with the cancer inside him he didn't feel very good, and probably working with wood helped to get his mind on something besides himself and his pain. Or perhaps he made it especially for Mom. Either way, the fact he gave it to her was a good thing.

Even if it was a random act of kindness, the fact it was strength and time spent from a man whose strength was waning and time was running out made it a most valuable gift. We used that little piece of furniture for years as a footstool in our living room, and I still have it to this very day.

Alfred died not too long after he gave us the gift. I would like to believe that there is a special place in heaven for people like Alfred Knoll. He had so many reasons to think only of himself or his young wife and daughter, and I know that he did. But for one afternoon or two, he made a gift for a widow and her children that was unsolicited.

A small inexpensive gift that is priceless to me.

CHAPTER ELEVEN

◆

1969

It didn't take my sister and me long before we were playing in vacant lots and walking down the street to play at other children's houses, just in the same way as the kids on Jackson Drive and 28th Street. Our dog Jeff never had any inhibitions about leaving the yard. Sometimes he was gone for three days before coming home (we just figured he'd found some female dogs to service). I've said earlier in this book Jeff was always the silent type, but apparently there were more important things on his list of things to do than bark. Where Jeff wandered remains a mystery. He was certainly going somewhere else other than to the seven houses on our block. My mom once thought he might have tried to return to the Alvis place. I will admit it took us awhile to get the hang of living in town.

Because Jeff was just a dog, obviously he'd never read the Bible, nor was he bound by the scriptures. At any rate, he certainly had no regard for that part of the Lord's Prayer about "forgive us our trespasses as we forgive those who trespass against us," because he was always "trespassing" somewhere or other (that was how the King James translation read, and was about the only translation used in the Sixties).

As for me, I took the "trespassing" part literally. To my mind when the Bible said "no trespassing," it meant it. In fact, when my ball would roll over in to someone's front yard, I didn't retrieve it without first walking over and ringing the door bell and asking permission to walk on their grass. I figured they might be looking out the window and would think less of me if I didn't get permission to trespass. I later realized that knocking on their door was more of an intrusion than quietly retrieving my ball.

Musically in 1969 things were still hot. The Who released—and toured—the first rock opera *Tommy*, opening the door to many other such works. As I've said, there had been a major change in popular music in the mid-1960s, and this was caused in part by the drug scene. This was exemplified by Captain Beefheart and his Magic Band (Frank Zappa's group) releasing the avant garde *Trout Mask Replica* that year. Acid rock, highly amplified and improvisational, and the more mellow psychedelic rock had gained prominence. When the Beatles turned to acid rock, their audience narrowed to the young.

A year earlier in 1968 the group Sly and the Family Stone had revolutionized black music with their massive hit single "Dance to the Music," and by 1969 they'd become international sensations with the release of their phenomenal hit record "Stand!" They then cemented their position as a vital counterculture band when they performed at the Woodstock Festival that summer, an event that for most represented the pinnacle of the hippie movement.

The festival was played before a crowd of nearly a half million-people gathered on a six-hundred acre spread called Yasgur's Farm, in upstate New York. Many top rock musicians were there, and it lasted three days, billing itself as a weekend of music, love and peace (even though the skies opened up and it rained like Noah's flood for most of it). The phenomenal music show drew over four hundred thousand hippies from all over the nation, and featured peace, love, and happiness ... and lots of LSD.

Although it was approaching the end, by 1969 the decade wasn't done with us yet. There was still more turmoil to come, chiefly from war protests and civil rights uprisings. President Richard Nixon had been inaugurated in January of that year and had promised "peace with honor" to end the Vietnam War; I don't think it worked. Plus under his presidency inflation soared, causing him to impose wage and price controls; I don't think that worked either.

I can't say that I remember Abbie Hoffman and the others who inspired the riots at the Democratic Convention in Chicago in 1968, or any other Vietnam protestors of the Sixties, by their faces. Some of their names are certainly familiar to me now, but I can't honestly say I was cognizant of them then. I do remember the fire hoses being turned on people, especially black folk, and the German shepherd police dogs growling and the National Guard troops and the tear gas. I never saw it in person, but we all saw it on the national news, both in the papers and on TV.

It had an impact on a lot of folks. Some were ashamed of what the establishment was doing to the civil protesters ("establishment" was a word the protestors like to use when referring to the government and the status quo). I for one looked at those protestors with a great deal of skepticism. I thought that anyone whose behavior required fire hoses or tear gas or police dogs was not credible.

I attributed the racial unrest to civil rights leader Martin Luther King, Jr. I don't remember ever hearing the famous "I have a dream" speech that he gave in Washington, DC in 1963 until I was an adult, but I considered him a trouble maker of the worst sort. I thought the fact that the fire hoses and the dogs were being used was evidence that what the protestors were asking for may have been a bridge too far, that more time was needed before they should be awarded everything they were asking for. Truth be told, I probably didn't even know back then what they were asking for.

And though it's hard to admit it, I have a bad confession to make. To my shame, I remember being glad when Reverend King was assassinated in Memphis, Tennessee on April 4, 1968. I ran outside and skipped when I heard he died.

I also wasn't too torn up when Senator Robert F. Kennedy followed him in assassination after being shot in the kitchen at the Ambassador Hotel in Los Angeles, California on June 5 of the same year. He died in the hospital the next morning. It is difficult to mourn for strangers sometimes, especially when you are ten years old.

I don't remember much about Bobby Kennedy except it seemed sad for the Kennedys to lose two boys so soon. I wondered if the same thing was going to happen to Teddy. I thought that maybe the country's troubles would stop with King now gone. But they didn't.

The blacks I knew never made trouble and I considered them my friends. But the blacks I saw on TV were very different. I was young and naïve back then, but I still have a dim view of the philosophy of the ends justifying the means. As a boy, I think I had an excuse for being blind to the trespasses of white folks, but in my eyes the riots on TV were nothing more than a blatant disrespect of authority.

In reality, of course, MLK was not as contentious as Abbie Hoffman, and certainly no trouble maker, but as a boy watching the outside world on TV, all the protesters seemed the same to me, no matter what their color. This was especially true of social activist and deputy chairman of the Illinois chapter of the Black Panther Party (BPP), Fred Hampton, who was assassinated that December.

The Black Panthers and the war protestors were unfathomable to someone like me who had watched glamorous movies of World War One and World War Two. I didn't know anything then about the falsehoods told about the gulf of Tonkin or the faults of LBJ, but I thought if freedom was for blacks, then it most certainly should be for the South Vietnamese too.

In Texas and across the Southwest there was another set of racial problems brewing that didn't get nearly the press the other stuff was getting. I'm talking about the Latino situation.

A lot of people hear it about now, with all the talk about illegal aliens, but back then it was pretty much confined to states like Texas, Arizona, New Mexico, and a couple others. Socially, the Chicano Movement addressed what it perceived to be negative ethnic stereotype of Mexicans in mass media and the American consciousness. It did so through the creation of works of literary and visual art that validated the Mexican-American ethnicity and culture.

The movement also addressed discrimination in public and private institutions. Early in the twentieth century, Mexican-Americans formed organizations to protect themselves from bias (as much as they could). One of those organizations, the League of United Latin American Citizens, was formed in 1929, and remains active today.

The movement gained momentum after World War II when groups such as the American G.I. Forum, which was formed by returning Mexican-American veterans, joined in the efforts by other civil rights organizations. As the century progressed, Mexican-American civil rights activists achieved several major legal victories. These included the 1947 *Mendez v. Westminster Supreme Court* ruling which declared that segregating children of "Mexican and Latin descent" was unconstitutional. Then in 1954 the *Hernandez v. Texas* ruling declared Mexican-Americans and other racial groups in the United States were entitled to equal protection under the 14th Amendment of the U.S. Constitution.

The most prominent civil rights organization in that particular community is the Mexican-American Legal Defense and Educational Fund (MALDEF), founded in 1968. Although modeled after the NAACP Legal Defense and Educational Fund, MALDEF also took on many of the functions of other organizations, including political advocacy and training of local leaders. During the 60s the number of Hispanic Americans tripled, and they became recognized as an oppressed minority. Also during this time activist Cesar Chavez organized Hispanics into the United Farm Workers Association.

1969 was also a huge year for the space program. On July 20 of that year, at 4:18 PM, one of the biggest events in history happened. Our spacecraft Apollo 11 landed on the moon, with astronauts Neil Armstrong and Buzz Aldrin aboard. And the best part was it was televised live to the watching world.

A few hours later when the lunar lander's hatch opened and Armstrong began to make his way down the ladder, we all watched, entranced. His famous words as he took the first historical steps on another world, "That's one small step for man, one giant leap for mankind," sent chills down my back. I've never forgotten it, and I doubt I ever will.

But getting back to the earth, and our dog Jeff: his incessant wandering once got him in trouble. One hot day he came home and lay down on the porch with his left front leg swollen up. Upon examining him we discovered Jeff had been bitten by either a rattlesnake or a copperhead (either one of which could easily kill a grown man, much less a dog).

For several days Jeff lay on the porch, motionless on the cool concrete, without food or water. His leg grew so big we thought it was going to pop. The vet said dogs had a way of knowing what to do, and told us just to let him lay on that cool concrete. After a few days of this, finally he managed to crawl a few feet to his water bowl we had put out for him and began to lap water. From then on, he slowly got better.

Jeff never changed his habits, and about a year later he walked off and never came back. We never found out what happened to him. He had never been in any close calls for trespassing as far as I knew, so I figured he was too smart to have reached his end that way. He had proven before that he knew how to survive a snake bite. I decided he knew he was going to die and he didn't want me to have to see it. I figured he went off for just that reason. That's when it hit me: the last creature to see my father alive was now dead.

Sometime after my father's death, Mammaw and Pappaw moved off their hundred-acre place on the banks of the Leon River at Ater to a small house near 19th and Saunders street in Gatesville. It was a complete surprise to everyone in the family. They sold the farm before any of their children even knew about it. We figured they didn't want anyone to fight over the place, so they sold it. Apparently Mammaw had talked Pappaw in to moving. His emphysema was getting worse, yet no one thought that he would ever leave the farm.

I remember years earlier when he explained to my dad that he had emphysema. Pappaw was sitting in a chair on the screened in porch and daddy was squatting on the ledge where the screen met the wall. I never knew anyone other than baseball catchers that could squat like that. I had tried to do it but it always killed my knees. I marveled how anyone not only endured it but preferred it as a comfortable relaxing position and with such balance.

Daddy was concerned and was listening and asking questions. Mammaw was just off the porch in the kitchen well within ear shot and would occasionally chime in as well. They said that Pappaw couldn't breathe because something was wrong with his lungs. They told Daddy that there was no cure and it was caused by his smoking cigarettes. Apparently Pappaw used to smoke them, although I had never seen him with anything but a pipe. They told us the doctor said all the physicians now knew about the dangers of smoking, but not anyone else. We even knew doctors that smoked, but they were getting less and less. The surgeon general had determined that smoking was a health hazard, and in 1965, had required cigarette manufacturers to start placing warnings on all packages and in all ads: "Smoking can be hazardous to your health". Until then it had not occurred to the US government to give out the warning that smoking could lead to cancer and lung problems.

Daddy relentlessly quizzed him about the accuracy of such a statement. Pappaw insisted the doctor told them that autopsies of smokers showed that their lungs were black, and that doctors themselves were beginning to quit smoking. Mammaw and Pappaw seemed resigned to the fact that there was no cure, but Daddy seemed concerned; I guess things like that take time to accept. Anyway, Daddy didn't live long enough to have to deal with it, at least not to the end.

Pappaw did not adjust to town life at all. I guess he had never lived in a town before. After supper and after dark, he used to strip down to his undershirt and boxers and go out on the porch and smoke his pipe. He continued this tradition in town as well. Mammaw used to holler at him to come back inside. He would reply that if she hadn't said anything no one would have known; after all, it was dark.

Things were fine until one evening Mammaw's sister Aunt Caddy came strolling up to the door after supper. All the fuss was for no good reason according to Pappaw. He stated that even in his underwear that he had on more clothes than most young women in their miniskirts.

Pappaw appeared to feel like a caged animal. He had nothing to do and nothing to look at. There was no river bottom land outside his porch, no neighbors he recognized driving past, no barn, no cows, no crops, no nothing. Just houses all bunched up together and town people rushing in and out of them with no real productivity occurring. He was suffocating in more ways than one.

I know he missed my dad. The first few years after my father's death we spent considerable time visiting my father's grave. As a matter of fact, my sister learned to spell our last name from looking at it on the tombstone. My mother would sit at the tombstone and cry a lot.

One time my great uncle Ruel walked over to the graveyard while we were there (Uncle Ruel was Pappaw's brother). He lived close by, but I think he had been over at the Timmons' who lived next to the graveyard and had spotted us over there. He gently talked to mom while she cried.

Now Ruel was a very different person. The rhythm of his speech and the whole way he spoke was almost like he was preaching. It was strange, but a good kind of strange. He would talk about Bible characters with a familiarity as if he knew them personally. He'd start with Abraham and continue on for some time. That day at the graveside every so often he would stop and quiz my mom to make sure she understood. It seemed to give her comfort.

Ruel was famous for asking a one-word question, "Savvy?" When one acknowledged in the affirmative, he would then say, "OK, tell me what I said." He was a very religious man, but in a more authentic way than most. He didn't go to our church, but the few times he visited there he spent most of the service bent over in prayer. Mammaw and Pappaw came to our church in town after we moved and after Pappaw died we brought Mammaw to church with us every Sunday.

Pappaw used to be bent over the whole service as well just like his brother Ruel. Some thought he was very religious and was in constant prayer too; perhaps he was, but I know for certain that with his emphysema he was bent over to get his breath. At his home, he often used a machine to give him enough oxygen. Pappaw coughed a lot at church. He coughed a lot everywhere, but it was more noticeable there. I had watched him for years all bent over at times, struggling to get enough oxygen. It was painful to see.

One night he came to our house on Royal Drive, and said he was going to try to put our new bookshelf together. He came alone, and he and I were in the living room while mom was working in the kitchen.

Prior to him pulling the metal bookshelf out of the box, he reviewed the books that were to be placed there. They were my dad's (and his son's) books, and included a set of Adam Clarke commentaries with pieces of paper placed inside containing Daddy's own notes. Some pages even had notes scribbled in the margins. There were also Bibles with notes stuffed inside and in the margins of the pages as well.

As he worked, Pappaw began to break down. When he did my mom walked in and asked him what was the matter. He mumbled that it wasn't fair for him to live and for his son to die. He said he was old and worn out and he should have been the one to die. Mom turned around and walked out of the room.

Pappaw began to remove all the parts out of the box and then started to fight with putting the pieces together ... and with himself. I wanted to help him but I was having a hard time understanding him, and he may have been too out of breath to repeat himself. If you recall, he spoke with a speech impediment, and with the crying he was difficult to understand. The closer he got to putting the bookcase together, the more he fell apart.

I went and got mom. She came back in the living room and tried to help him, but he was to the point he couldn't see for the tears and couldn't hold anything in his hands. Mom told him that she could finish putting it together later. He ignored her. He continued to try but he just couldn't.

Finally, he heeded my mom's plea that she would finish it later. She went back to the kitchen and before she could rustle up some supper, he left dejected. He probably was in a hurry to get home to Mammaw also. I had been glad that he was coming over and was looking forward to a pleasant evening, but that was not to be.

In February 1969 he died, within six months after moving to town. Everyone said the emphysema had killed him, but town life appeared to be the final nail in the coffin. I think he would have lived much longer had he stayed on the river.

He had a strength about him. He was a good man.

I miss him.

CHAPTER TWELVE

●

EPILOGUE

There is a joke that tells about a group of blind men that were led out to an elephant. One felt the trunk and said that an elephant was like a snake; a couple of them felt the legs and agreed that an elephant was like a tree trunk. And one felt the reproductive parts and was trampled to death by the elephant. The Sixties may be like that elephant. All of us that lived back then experienced it differently, as if we were blind. Some were flower children, or better known as hippies. Some were nerds, because there are nerds in every generation. Some were rednecks. Some were other classifications. Some eventually were destroyed by drugs and the so-called sexual revolution. But all of us were human. We all made mistakes. We all lived and loved and laughed and experienced heartaches and sadness. We all were oppressors and we all were oppressed. The decades roll on and we think that things are worse than they have ever been before or better than they have ever been before. Neither is correct. Someone once said that life is what you do while you are reacting to what you didn't plan for. We are as blind now as we were back then, perhaps in different ways or on different issues.

I chose a decade that was difficult and easy for me to write about. It was difficult because I was very young and I have more recent memories of the seventies, eighties, nineties, and this new century. It was easy because my roots and foundation were set in the Sixties. I want people to know that rednecks are more than caricatures such as the characters like Larry the Cable guy or personalities presented by Jeff Foxworthy. I want folks to know that rednecks are not stupid or lazy or ignorant. Sweeping generalizations about any group of people is fraught with opportunities to make great miscalculations that can cause harm to them, and to the one thinking of them. Sometimes that harm consists of missed opportunities to connect with another human being.

I want to contribute to that long line of storytellers that have told tales for centuries. Story telling is something that men in particular like to do. Listening to a good story is enjoyable, and telling one is too. There is a saying, "Never let the truth get in the way of a good story." I have been known for hyperbole and for tall tales, but truth has always been very important to me, and I've tried very hard to tell this story straight. I left out most of my very best friends and my worst enemies (I really don't remember an enemy except myself at times). Some things don't need repeating because mountains don't need to be made out of mole hills, and some mountains need to be climbed in private. I chose a decade that most say was tumultuous. Perhaps my soul was placed in a bag of flesh on the North American continent to be a boy during that decade so I could write to you about those tumultuous times.

As you have read, I was just another blind person, a very young blind person at that, trying to feel my way around. I think that is true for all rednecks or nerds, or hippies, or any other category of humans. We all have to feel our way around, and unless you are God, you can't truly see what you are doing, or know what you are doing to your self or to others. Most of us have some idea, but none of us see the unintended consequences of our actions, although God warns us about it in the Ten Commandments written in Exodus chapter 20, verse 5. He states that he is a jealous God, and that he will punish the children for the sins of the fathers to the third and fourth generation, and that he will show love to a thousand generations of them that love him and keep his commandments.

Actions have consequences. They always have and they always will. We all have tendencies toward worship of some kind. Perhaps it's not actual golden calves, but even though we may attend church, we face the temptation to have a proverbial "golden calf" in our life that dominates our activities and our time. The Sixties did not happen in a vacuum, and to borrow another phrase, "no man is an island".

One metaphor that seems to work is that mankind sits on a three-legged stool (the three-legged stool proverb has been used many times throughout history, and this version, though not original, differs from most you have heard before; I don't actually remember what parts I acquired, and how much of it may be my own adaptation). The first leg is our societal or cultural underpinning. The next leg is our political underpinning. And last but not least the final leg is our religious underpinning.

In my opinion, the societal and political legs are heavily influenced by the religious underpinning (or the lack thereof). Others have argued that society contains political and religious elements and they are the same leg.

I contend that the physical world is the world that society gravitates to, and all governments except theocracies attempt to stand in the physical world also. Governments are separate from culture, although they heavily influence each other. The religious leg stands in the spiritual world and influences all, and often time is temporarily influenced by society and politics.

The events and actions of the USA in the Sixties were the result of those legs being out of balance for what ever reason. The Sixties were tumultuous due to blessings and punishments for our short comings and/or the blessings and punishments of our forefathers.

Technology drives social change. TV and automobiles are great examples, but they were not invented in the Sixties. Businesses can drive social change, and technology and business are intertwined. Many families left the farms during the Sixties, which was a social change largely due to both technological advances and political influences.

There were other dramatic societal changes in clothing and personal appearance in the Sixties because we forgot the reasons for the norms that were in place. Perhaps scriptures used as proof text about men not wearing long hair were misinterpreted; perhaps not. How about the ones talking about men and women not wearing each other clothes? Yes, there are scriptures in the Bible about cross dressing (which begs the question: are women cross dressing if they wear pants?).

These issues came up during the Sixties and seventies and were probably founded in the confusion and carelessness that occurred in the Fifties. Religious traditions for tradition's sake are not good reasons to do them. The problem now is that we do not have answers, because the truth is we have long forgotten the questions. Each generation, each decade becomes preoccupied with some other imbalance of the three-legged stool.

Political unrest regarding civil rights most definitely could be chickens coming home to roost (punishment) for sins of our forefathers regarding slavery. (I wrote this down long before I ever heard of Jeremiah Wright.) Perhaps the Vietnam War became unpopular because of our lackadaisical view of communism created by our failure to appreciate the messages of "Tailgunner" Joe McCarthy, and of then-Congressman Richard Nixon during his Alger Hiss days (not to mention the incompetence of President Lyndon Johnson to wage that war). The American electorate swung from Ike to Kennedy and LBJ and then back to Nixon, trying to once again keep the proverbial stool in balance.

Too often we fail to heed the message because we find fault with the messenger and quickly dismiss the validity of his argument. Certainly, America has been blessed by the actions of our forefathers who created this nation, hopefully for at least a thousand more generations.

Last but not least, the religious leg was absent at times. For instance, when President Johnson instituted the "Great Society," where were the religious leaders of our nation? James 1:27 states "Religion that God our Father accepts as pure and faultless is this: to look after orphans and widows in their distress and to keep oneself from being polluted by the world."

Why didn't the religious leaders in our nation say "Mr. President don't worry, we will step up to the task."? If one truly advocates separation of church and state, then why should the state be doing the church's business? Once again, the political leg was compensating for the religious leg.

Galatians chapter 5 verse 1 reads. "It is for freedom that Christ has set us free." The societal leg and the political leg would interpret that freedom as self rule, thus saying "It is for *self rule* that Christ has set us free." But the religious leg interprets freedom as a relationship with God, thus saying "It is for *a relationship with God* that Christ has set us free." And that, folks, that latter one is the truth.

The Sixties were often filled with religious leaders arguing over form of worship instead of relationship, while others in society and political circles were arguing over self rule. Both were wrong, and both caused us harm.

How does all this philosophy have to do with the rest of this book? A lot of politics and religion have been flung out after reading about a boy in the Sixties, a boy who arguably lived a very sheltered life, and was not extremely cognizant of the world around him.

Yet it may have been a time in my life when I was closest to innocence. I was a boy who all at Stanley Chapel predicted would be a preacher or a politician. I was a boy who grew up and has been laughed at (and laughed with) for being a redneck. I have called myself, and have been called by others, the "quintessential redneck."

I pray that my pride in rural lifestyle, my pride in having liberty in government (not to be confused with liberal/progressive politics) and my pride in anything else has not blinded me more than what I am already. Because no matter if we are nerds, or hippies, or any other classification, what we should take pride in is Christ crucified and resurrected, in being a Christian.

From a religious standpoint, and that is the most important leg, my label is simply "Christian." From a political standpoint; my label is something in the Republican spectrum; perhaps a pragmatic libertarian is a more fitting title. But from a social or cultural perspective I am guilty as charged; the quintessential redneck.

Printed in the United States
By Bookmasters